HOW TO KEEP YOUR CHOLESTEROL
IN CHECK

DR ROBERT POVEY is a writer and lecturer, and former Psychology at Christ Church College, Canterbury. also a qualified nurse. He has written several scientific papers and books on topics in psychology, health and education and is a Fellow of the British Psychological Society. As part of his background research for the book Dr Povey interviewed a wide range of people with cholesterol problems, and the text is based on genuine case histories. Having had to cope personally with the need to modify cholesterol levels by diet, he has also gained valuable first-hand experience of the problems involved in keeping cholesterol in check.

Overcoming Common Problems Series

Selected titles

A full list of titles is available from Sheldon Press,
36 Causton Street, London SW1P 4ST and on our website at
www.sheldonpress.co.uk

Overcoming Common Problems

HOW TO KEEP YOUR CHOLESTEROL IN CHECK

Dr Robert Povey

First published in Great Britain in 1994
Sheldon Press
36 Causton Street
London SW1P 4ST

British Library Cataloguing in Publication Data
A catalogue record for this book is available from the British Library

ISBN 0–85969–776–2

9 10 8

Photoset by Deltatype Ltd, Ellesmere Port, Cheshire
Printed and bound in Great Britain by Biddles Ltd, King's Lynn, Norfolk

Contents

Acknowledgements

I am indebted to the many people who have given their time to talk to me about their cholesterol problems and ways of coping with them; and also to a variety of medical experts, nutritionists, and dietitians.

In particular, I would like to thank Professor Tony Winder of the Royal Free Hospital, London, together with Dr Michael Turner and Linda Convery, formerly Chief Executive and specialist dietitian, respectively, with the FHA, for their generous help and advice during the writing of the book, and for commenting on the manuscript; I am also most grateful to the following people for providing information and discussing ideas at various stages of the project: Dr Gilbert Thompson (MRC Lipoprotein Team, Hammersmith Hospital), Professor Tom Sanders (King's College, University of London), Jacqui Lynas (Specialist Lipid Dietitian, HEART UK and Hastings and Rother NHS Trust), Professor Hugh Tunstall-Pedoe (University of Dundee), Professor Gerry Shaper (Royal Free Hospital, London), Dr Tony Keech (University of Oxford), Dr Michael Laker (University of Newcastle upon Tyne), Dr John Reckless (Royal United Hospital, Bath), Dr Mike Rayner (Coronary Prevention Group), Belinda Linden (British Heart Foundation), and Victoria Fitch (Health Education Authority).

I would also like to thank my own GP, Dr James Lorimer, and Practice Nurse Betty Flint, for their clinical expertise, and for the encouragement and advice they have given at each stage in the book's progress; Dr David Cox, for his help with background research; Libby Nichols, for tasting recipes and reading the manuscript; Sue Cover (Librarian at the Postgraduate Medical Centre, Kent and Canterbury Hospital), for her assistance in tracking down research papers; Joanna Moriarty (Editorial Director, SPCK), for getting the book off the ground, making some extremely valuable comments on the first draft, and steering it through to publication; and my daughter, Rachel, for helping with some of the early interviews and for commenting on the text. Finally, I wish to thank my wife, Lyn, for her invaluable advice at every stage of the project, and for her constant support and encouragement.

Foreword

Coronary heart disease is *the* public health priority in most developed countries. Of particular concern are the many who suffer angina, coronary bypass operations or heart attack while still relatively young. The disease is caused by the combined effects of a number of risk factors which cause premature degeneration of the heart and circulatory system. When several risk factors combine, the chances of a person developing coronary heart disease are much increased.

The best known of the risk factors is raised blood cholesterol. Cholesterol contributes to the formation of plaque which can narrow the small coronary arteries that feed the heart muscle itself; and it combines with other risk factors such as high blood pressure, high blood glucose level, smoking, an inactive lifestyle and obesity to produce damaging effects on the heart and circulatory system.

Anyone with raised blood cholesterol will benefit from its reduction, whether from a massively elevated level as in inherited disorders such as familial hypercholesterolaemia (FH), or from a more modest level. There is a direct relationship between cholesterol level and risk of heart disease: the higher the cholesterol the higher the risk, the lower the cholesterol, the lower the risk. Hence, personal management of blood cholesterol is a must for everyone seeking better heart-health.

This book is a good guide to the successful management of cholesterol and the associated lifestyle changes which will help to reduce heart disease and promote good health. These include taking regular exercise, eating plenty of vegetables, cereals and fruits, and learning to relax, while limiting smoking, drinking, body weight and blood pressure.

HEART UK (formerly the Family Heart Association) is a support organization committed to raising awareness of the dangers of high cholesterol and stressing the importance of diet, lifestyle and clinical expertise in controlling cholesterol and in the reduction of coronary heart disease risk. *How to Keep Your Cholesterol in Check* is based on the personal experiences of people with cholesterol problems and provides a valuable source of information and ideas in line with these objectives.

Many books on health and nutrition are confusing, distorted, or, all too often, wrong. It is refreshing, therefore, to find a book which is reliable and easy to read. It will be useful to health professionals as well as their patients or members of the public seeking to understand cholesterol and its role in coronary heart disease.

Dr Michael Turner
Formerly Chief Executive, Family Heart Association

Preface to the Second Edition

For most people the best way of keeping cholesterol in check is to follow the sort of lifestyle and dietary advice contained in Chapters 7–10. These have been updated to take account of changes in current thinking about diet, appropriate levels of exercise and advice on 'sensible drinking' in relation to alcohol. Such guidelines are by no means simply 'denial' regimes in which, for example, what you eat is determined by what you can't have! The aim is to concentrate on the range and variety of foods and activities which are enjoyable and satisfying in themselves but will also help to keep cholesterol in check and contribute to a general improvement in quality of life. For some people, however, diet and lifestyle measures alone will not be sufficient to control cholesterol problems and medication may be necessary. The types of drugs described in the first edition still represent the main forms of medication used in the treatment of cholesterol problems but some important large scale research studies have been carried out on their effectiveness. These studies emphasize, in particular, the extent to which the risk of heart attacks can be reduced by 30 to 40 per cent by using appropriate medication. The findings are discussed in Chapter 11. The remainder of the text has also been modified where necessary to take account of new research and practice in the management of cholesterol problems.

1

A typical case

John is an energetic, capable, and enthusiastic sales director in his mid-fifties. Although he smokes several cigarettes a day, he eats and sleeps well, plays the occasional game of golf, hardly ever goes to his doctor, and doesn't think he needs a check-up because he feels so fit. His wife, on the other hand, is much more 'health conscious', and has been trying for some time to persuade John to follow her example and go to the surgery for a routine health check. She points out that he takes the family car for its regular service in order to keep it in good running order, to prolong its life, and to deal with any minor problems before they become major ones, so why won't he do the same for his own body?

Although John can see the essential thrust of his wife's argument, he has in the past shrugged off her suggestions. Finally, though, her persuasive arguments – and the fact that one of his colleagues (about John's age) recently suffered a minor heart attack – have convinced John that a check-up might be a good idea. He has, therefore, agreed to book an appointment at the surgery on the understanding that the check-up would be carried out at a 'Well Person' clinic!

Having made the appointment, the receptionist asked John to ensure that he came to the session without having eaten or drunk anything (except water) for the previous 12 hours. This suggestion rather horrified John (since he is particularly fond of his supper-time snack!), and he asked the receptionist if this was absolutely essential. 'Oh, yes,' she replied, 'it's for your cholesterol check – we do a proper fasting test here.' John was rapidly going off the idea of the check-up, but reluctantly agreed to the conditions.

During John's overall 'screening' session, the nurse completed a checklist for such things as height, weight, smoking and drinking habits, history of illnesses in the family and tested his blood pressure and urine. Finally, she came to the 'fasting test' and took a blood sample, explaining that this was to check John's blood cholesterol. She also explained that some of the blood fats (lipids) tend to be raised for a few hours after a meal, so it was best to do the test when the body had been starved for a 12-hour period. John found that it was all completed very simply and painlessly, and as he rolled down

1

his sleeve afterwards he felt very pleased with himself for having attended the check-up.

A week later, John rang the surgery and was advised that he ought to come in to see the doctor concerning his results. He was informed that it was nothing serious, but that his cholesterol level was a little raised. At his appointment, John was told by the doctor, 'Your cholesterol level is 7.2 – a bit on the high side. It's nothing to worry about, but we'd prefer you to be around the 5.2 mark. You'll need to go on a diet to see if we can reduce it – cut down on the saturated fats, no fry-ups for breakfast! And it would help if you gave up smoking, too. Anyway, pop in and see the nurse – she'll give you a diet sheet, and we'll see you again in three months for another check.'

John felt a bit aggrieved by this news – he enjoyed his fried breakfast, his cream cake snacks and his cigarettes. He knew that he was a bit overweight and that he ought to stop smoking, but thought that everything was OK because he felt so well. John knew that smoking was likely to affect his lungs (and possibly his heart) in the long run, but why did this have anything to do with cholesterol? And what is cholesterol anyway?

2
What is cholesterol?

The nature of cholesterol

Cholesterol is frequently seen as something entirely harmful with headlines concentrating on the relationship between high levels of cholesterol in the blood and increased risk of heart disease. However, it is important to appreciate that cholesterol also has a friendly (and indeed vital) role to play in maintaining the healthy functioning of our bodies. These are its main functions:

- it provides an essential component of the membrane of every cell in our bodies;
- it is used to make bile[1]; this green-coloured liquid is stored in the gall bladder and plays an important role in the digestion of fatty foods;
- it is a building block in the production of hormones that are essential to life;
- it is one of the raw materials our bodies need to make vitamin D;
- it helps to insulate our nerves, and may provide a sort of 'waterproofing' agent in the linings of arteries.

So cholesterol is certainly not all bad – in fact, we cannot live without it!

The texture of cholesterol is soft and waxy, with a consistency something like warm candle-grease. This yellowish-white, fatty substance is for the most part manufactured by our own bodies, in the liver. About two-thirds of the body's cholesterol is produced in this way, using substances derived from the fat in our food. Hence, the more fat we eat,the more cholesterol the liver is encouraged to make. This is particularly true in relation to eating *saturated fat*; this is found in lots of food, but mostly in foods derived from animal sources, e.g. full-cream milk and fatty meat or cheese. The remaining cholesterol in our bodies comes by a different route, mainly from the wall of the small intestine as a result of fats that we eat, or, to a lesser extent (about 10 per cent), from cholesterol in food (i.e. what is called *dietary cholesterol*). This dietary cholesterol is only found in foods of animal origin such as meat, egg yolks, fish-roe, and some shellfish, and its role is relatively insignificant in the development of cholesterol problems. The main culprit when problems arise from unbalanced eating habits is almost always an excessive intake of saturated fat.

Cholesterol is one of a number of fats (called *lipids*) that are carried in the bloodstream. Our bodies coat the lipids with a special protein to make them water-soluble.[2] Then these tiny protein-coated particles (called *lipoproteins*) are carried in the blood to the cells. When fat (lipid) levels in general are too high, we are said to have *hyperlipidaemia*; and when cholesterol levels in particular are raised, the condition is called *hypercholesterolaemia*.

LDL and HDL

The main cholesterol-carrying lipoproteins are known as LDL (low density lipoprotein) and HDL (high density lipoprotein). Over two-thirds of the cholesterol in our blood is of the LDL variety and its main function is to collect and transport cholesterol around the body to the cells.[3] Unfortunately, when LDL cholesterol is found in excessive amounts, it produces deposits that fur up our arteries, restricting the blood supply. This condition is called *atherosclerosis*. This restriction in blood supply can lead to *angina* (pain in the chest on exertion or when over-excited), and sometimes to an un-expectedly sudden *thrombosis* (the formation of a blood clot).

The primary function of HDL, on the other hand, is potentially much more friendly. It seems likely that it acts a bit like a scavenger, collecting up surplus cholesterol from the arteries and taking it back again to the liver. Safely back in the liver, this cholesterol can be reprocessed or turned into bile. Therefore we need to be looking for ways of increasing the proportion of our HDL 'good guys' as a protective measure against the damaging effects of the excess LDL 'bad guys'. As one person put it in a Family Heart Association newsletter: 'The HDL are "*H*ighly *D*esirable" and the LDL are "*L*ess *D*esirable".'

Triglycerides

These fats are carried around the bloodstream by what are called VLDL (very low density lipoprotein). As with cholesterol, triglyceride is either made in the liver or comes from fat in foods that we eat. The body's production of triglyceride is also stimulated by an increased intake of refined carbohydrate (sugar) in the diet, especially in the form of alcohol. Triglyceride constitutes an important source of energy for our bodies, but in excess may lead to an increased tendency for the blood to form clots. Thus, people who have raised levels of triglyceride (*hypertriglyceridaemia*) tend to have a greater risk of developing coronary heart disease.

Heart disease: some technical terms explained

Since atherosclerosis can result in all sorts of problems in what's called the *cardio-vascular system* (the heart and its related blood vessels), it might be useful at this point to explain a few of the other medical terms that you may come across.

For example, a thrombosis that occurs in a coronary artery or one of its branches usually leads to a heart attack (sometimes referred to as a *coronary*). This means part of the heart muscle is deprived of sustenance and will die (technically known as *myocardial infarction* or *MI*) unless the clot can be removed within a very short time after its occurrence. You will find that the term coronary heart disease is often shortened to *CHD*, and it may also be called *ischaemic* heart disease.

The term *stroke* is used to describe a thrombosis that occurs in the brain (i.e. a *cerebral thrombosis*), and it can also describe damage to the brain caused in other ways. For example, the rupture of one of the brain's arteries (a *cerebral haemorrhage*) is described as a stroke, as also is the situation in which an artery has been blocked as a result of debris, such as blood clots that have reached the brain from other parts of the body – often from the heart. This latter form of stroke is also known as a *cerebral embolism*. All these events can be triggered off by an excess of LDL cholesterol, and the resultant atherosclerosis.

Having looked very briefly at the nature of cholesterol and the other blood fats, we now need to turn to John's other question: what has cholesterol to do with other things like smoking? To examine this, we need to look at the concept of risk factors.

3

Risk factors:
the research evidence

If you decided to take out a life insurance policy for a fairly large sum of money, you might be asked by the insurance company to have a medical examination. The purpose of this would be to assess your chances of living to a ripe old age or of dying prematurely. In the latter case, the company would find themselves considerably out of pocket, since you would have paid only a small amount of money by way of your insurance premiums – whereas they would be obliged to make a substantial pay-out! So before they agree to take you on, they are keen to assess the degree of risk that they are incurring; and in order to do this, they will examine a number of risk factors. These factors include any genetic or environmental factors that are known to increase the chances of an individual developing certain diseases and reducing life expectancy. In relation to heart disease, one of these risk factors is raised total cholesterol level and another is smoking – hence the link between cholesterol and smoking in the medical examination.

For the purposes of the present discussion, the concept of risk factors will be confined for the most part to those characteristics that increase an individual's chances of developing coronary heart disease (CHD) and, in general, the greater the number of risk factors, the greater the level of risk. The main risk factors for coronary heart disease are related to:

1 blood pressure
2 smoking
3 cholesterol
4 inactivity
5 obesity
6 stress
7 fibrinogen
8 family history
9 diabetes
10 gender
11 age
12 country of origin.

The interaction of risk factors

In considering these risk factors, it is very important to keep in mind that heart disease isn't usually caused by one factor alone, but by the interaction of several factors – and when a person has more than one risk factor, the chances of having a heart attack (or possibly a stroke) are far more than marginally increased. If you're a smoker, for example, then your risk of having a heart attack is doubled when compared with someone who is a non-smoker, and as each additional risk factor is added, the chances of developing heart disease are multiplied again. This means that a person with three of the major risk factors (e.g. a smoker with raised blood pressure and high total cholesterol) will have something like eight times the chance of having a heart attack (i.e. $2 \times 2 \times 2$) compared with the person without these risk factors.

We will consider in the next chapter which people are most at risk from having raised cholesterol scores, and in Chapter 5 we will look more closely at the ways in which overall risk scores can be calculated. First, though, we must look at the sort of research evidence used in the identification of risk factors, and how this evidence relates to each separate factor.

Typical research studies

Most of the research that has helped to identify the major risk factors for heart disease (including cholesterol) comes from large-scale studies in which thousands of people have been subjected to repeated medical checks and an examination of their lifestyles over a long period of time. One of the most famous studies is the Framingham Heart Study, which began in the late 1940s. About 5,000 men and women between the ages of 30 and 59 in Framingham, Massachusetts, agreed to take part in a study that involved the participants having regular medical checks every two years. The study confirmed, for example, the relationship between smoking and coronary heart disease (CHD), and indicated that people with raised cholesterol levels had a higher risk of a heart attack, angina, or a stroke. Similarly, it drew attention to the way in which risk factors such as smoking, raised blood pressure, and high cholesterol act together to multiply the chances of any individual developing coronary heart disease. A similar type of study, the British Regional Heart Study, involving nearly 8,000 men aged

7

between 40 and 59, also confirms the link between high cholesterol and increased risk of coronary heart disease; and the Scottish Heart Health Study, involving over 10,000 people (half men and half women) aged 40 to 59, has provided further valuable data on the prevalence and levels of risk factors in Scotland, a country that has a particularly bad record for heart disease.

One study, called the Seven Countries Study, provides an important international perspective on the relative importance of risk factors in the development of heart disease. The research began in the 1950s and involved studying over 12,000 men between the ages of 40 and 59 in seven different countries: the USA, Japan, Yugoslavia (as it was then), Finland, Italy, Greece and the Netherlands. There are problems, of course, in trying to make comparisons between countries because of the many variables involved, but the findings tell us some interesting things about the possible relationship between diet and heart disease, and they also demonstrate a clear relationship between heart disease and raised cholesterol. For the Finnish men, for example, 56 per cent of whom had raised total cholesterol levels, the incidence of heart attack was about 13 times as high over a ten-year period as for their Japanese counterparts, only seven per cent of whom had raised levels.

The evidence from these (and many other) large-scale research studies offers strong support for the view that heart disease is the result of a number of interacting factors, including heredity, life-style, and diet. It is true that a number of influential research studies have been criticized for having design flaws or making unwarranted and excessive claims for the influence of cholesterol as a risk factor, but the weight of evidence accumulated from around the world shows that the risk of coronary heart disease tends to increase with a rise in blood cholesterol levels, just as it does with raised blood pressure and smoking.

The increasing availability of techniques that allow doctors to see what is actually happening in the arteries has helped to refine our understanding of the role of risk factors in heart disease. Some techniques, such as *angiography*, have been around for some time. This is when a small catheter is passed through an artery into the heart so that the coronary arteries can be examined directly. The resulting picture on the screen or photograph, called an angiogram, will show exactly what is happening in the arteries. Similarly, the more recently developed *Magnetic Resonance Imaging* technique (MRI) will show images of the arteries and nerves, and this offers further scope for sophisticated investigations into heart disease. Such techniques have helped to demonstrate that a reduction in levels of cholesterol in the blood can prevent the plaques from increasing, and in some cases can lead to a reduction ('regression') of existing plaques.

The evidence for each risk factor

Before we look at each risk factor in turn, it's worth making the point that the first five factors can be eliminated or greatly reduced by lifestyle changes that we can make. This is the good news – for even if you are genetically predisposed to develop cholesterol problems, your diet and lifestyle still play a major role in determining whether and to what extent these problems are allowed to take hold. So if you do have a few unwelcome risk factors at the moment, remember that you can do something about them, and this book aims to show you how.

1 Blood pressure

Blood pressure (often referred to simply as BP) is the pressure of the blood against the artery walls. It is measured by the height in millimetres (mm Hg) that a column of mercury reaches when your blood pressure is checked. When you have your blood pressure tested, an inflatable cuff is put around your upper arm; this cuff is then inflated until it cuts off the blood flow in your arm. The air in the cuff is then slowly released until the pulse returns and can be heard through the stethoscope. This is when the upper (*systolic*) pressure is noted, and this indicates the maximum pressure the heart is using to pump blood round the body. Next the cuff is further deflated and the minimum, or lower (*diastolic*) pressure is taken. The systolic pressure can vary quite markedly depending on physical, mental, or emotional exertion, whereas the diastolic pressure tends to remain more constant. It can be argued, therefore, that the diastolic measurement (the lower figure) is likely to offer a slightly more reliable guide to the presence of blood pressure problems than the systolic pressure. When doctors refer to blood pressure measurements, you'll find they usually give the systolic score first and then the diastolic – so that 'BP 120/80' means that the systolic level is 120 mm Hg and the diastolic level is 80 mm Hg.

Both the Framingham Heart Study and the British Regional

Heart Study found that people having high blood pressure (called hypertension) had two to three times the risk of having a heart attack compared with people with blood pressure in the normal range; and for people in the hypertensive range, there is an even greater risk of having a stroke. The World Health Organization defines raised blood pressure as:

- above 160 mm Hg systolic and 95 mm Hg diastolic.

In practice there seems to be general consensus that blood pressure readings that are consistently around 150–160 mm Hg for systolic blood pressure, and 90–95 mm Hg for diastolic blood pressure, require careful monitoring. (The usual sort of range in people without blood pressure problems would be somewhere between 100 and 140 systolic and 60 to 90 diastolic.) In both the Framingham and Scottish studies, levels of 160/95 mm Hg were used to classify people with high blood pressure, but in the British Regional Heart Study a twofold increase in risk of heart disease was noted at slightly lower levels – when the systolic pressure was in excess of 148 mm Hg and diastolic above 93 mm Hg.

There are several factors that affect blood pressure levels, of course, and these need to be considered when interpreting scores and taking preventative measures. For example, blood pressure tends to be higher in men, and rises with age. High blood pressure is also associated with smoking, obesity, stress, excess alcohol intake, and salt consumption; and although we can't do much about our gender or age, we can lower blood pressure by reducing these other factors. Keeping fit by aerobic exercise (the sort that gets you slightly puffed, like brisk walking or jogging) and by paying attention to diet (e.g. snacking on fruit instead of salty crisps, and keeping alcohol intake to within sensible limits) will also help lower blood pressure. It has been calculated, for example, that a reduction in diastolic pressure of 6–8 mm Hg could be associated with a 25 per cent reduction in the incidence of coronary heart disease and a 50 per cent reduction in strokes. So it is clear that even minor changes in lifestyle are capable of producing major changes in life expectancy! (Suggestions on diet and exercise will be covered more fully in Chapters 7, 8, and 9.)

2 Smoking

Smoking is one of the major risk factors for both coronary heart disease and stroke, in addition to its connection with various cancers (it is the cause of most cancers of the lung, trachea, larynx, mouth, and oesophagus). The findings from the Framingham Heart Study and the British Regional Heart Study, for example, suggest that smoking is associated with a coronary heart disease risk level two and three times greater than that for a non-smoker, depending on the amount of tobacco smoked. It has also been calculated that smoking accounts for up to 18 per cent of deaths from coronary heart disease and 11 per cent of stroke deaths – and, of course, the risk of coronary heart disease is multiplied when smoking is associated with other risk factors. Since smoking is associated with higher concentrations of fibrinogen (another risk factor that is discussed later) in the blood, this is rather like building in a quadrupled risk factor from the start! Smokers also tend to have lower HDL's than non-smokers and slightly higher triglyceride levels, both of which increase their risk of heart disease. According to the Seven Countries Study the most severe threat from smoking is likely to occur in Western countries such as the UK, where average blood cholesterol levels tend to be on the high side anyway. The risk is also increased further for women smokers taking oral contraceptives.

So it's clear that smoking is bad news for the smoker, but there is an increasing amount of evidence to suggest that 'passive smoking' (the inhalation of other people's smoke), carries similar (though smaller) risks to those affecting active smokers. For example, there is evidence that fibrinogen levels are increased in people exposed to passive smoking at home or at work, and that children of parents who smoke have a higher risk of developing respiratory ailments. Also, smoking during pregnancy increases the risks of stillbirth, miscarriage, and low birth weight.

If we look on the positive side, though, smoking is a risk factor that it is possible to reverse more or less completely, so that the level of risk of someone who gives up smoking is reduced to that of a person who has never smoked. In calculating scores for an ex-smoker, the Dundee Coronary Risk Disk (to be described in Chapter 5) reduces the excess risk over a 'never smoker' to half, two years after stopping. After three years this drops to a third, and to the level of a 'never smoker' after ten years. So if you are a smoker it makes good sense to stop as soon as possible in order to reverse the bad effects. There are several approaches to giving up smoking, including the use of nicotine replacement therapy. For most smokers, though, giving up is usually accomplished without such pharmacological help, and some advice on how to stop is offered in Chapter 10. There are also a number of helpful booklets and videos prepared by organizations such as ASH (Action on Smoking and Health) – see the Useful Addresses section on p.121.

3 Cholesterol

Raised cholesterol is associated with an increased risk of heart disease and gallstones, and it has been estimated that a 10 per cent reduction in total cholesterol level in populations where the average level is raised, could result in something like a 20–30 per cent reduction in death from coronary heart disease within a five-year period.

In the UK, where heart disease and strokes account for two in every five deaths, it is calculated that about a fifth of the population have high-risk levels on at least three of the first four factors in our list (blood pressure, smoking, cholesterol, and inactivity). As far as cholesterol is concerned, surveys indicate that over two-thirds of the population have cholesterol readings above the desirable level, a finding that relates to both men and women. It is, therefore, of crucial importance that the benefits of lowering cholesterol levels are recognized. According to one major study involving over half a million people, a reduction of 0.6 mmol/l in total cholesterol level can result in a decrease in risk of coronary heart disease by as much as 50 per cent. The findings can be summarized in the following way:

- A ten per cent reduction in blood cholesterol produces a reduction in risk of coronary heart disease of 50 per cent at age 40, 40 per cent at age 50, 30 per cent at age 60, and 20 per cent at age 70+. This benefit would be seen relatively quickly – the greater part within two years and the full benefit after five years.

In the next chapter we will consider possible 'screening' approaches that will enable people with severe cholesterol problems to be identified and treated at an early stage, then in Chapter 5 we will look at what constitutes 'a raised cholesterol level'. For now, though, we simply need to be aware that raised cholesterol level is an important risk factor in heart disease, but one that is amenable to treatment.

4 Inactivity

Inactivity or lack of exercise is increasingly becoming recognized as an important risk factor for heart disease. Several studies have found that people who regularly take a moderate amount of brisk exercise will tend to have fewer heart attacks and strokes later on in life than people who are inactive. The British Regional Heart Study, for example, found the risk of stroke in middle-aged men to be over six times as great for inactive men as for those who took vigorous exercise, with an intermediate level of risk for men taking light exercise. This association between inactivity and high risk of stroke was also seen, even when allowance was made for the other factors that tend to be linked to an inactive lifestyle – such as obesity and high blood pressure. Regular exercise may also protect against the age-related increase in blood pressure that tends to be a characteristic of middle-aged people within Western societies. Blood pressure does, of course, tend to rise during the actual period of exercise itself, but what seems to happen is that regular activity helps to keep the heart and its related blood vessels (the cardio-vascular system) in good shape. This means that the whole system works more efficiently – the blood vessels are more elastic, the heart has to work less hard to pump the blood around the body, and consequently blood pressure and pulse rate tend to come down.

Lack of exercise as a risk factor for women is less clearly defined, partly because fewer large-scale studies have been carried out with female subjects. Smaller-scale studies, however, have established that women do reap the same benefits as men from the ability of exercise to lower blood pressure, raise the 'good' HDL cholesterol, and help in controlling weight. It seems likely, therefore, that women can help to lower their levels of risk in the same way as men by exercising regularly.

The general guideline is to try to exercise for about 30 minutes at least five days a week by engaging in a moderately intense form of physical activity such as swimming, brisk walking, or playing a sport that is energetic enough to get you slightly out of breath.

5 Obesity

The Framingham Heart Study showed that men between the ages of 35 and 44, whose weight was ten per cent above that which would be considered 'normal' for their height, had a 38 per cent higher risk of developing heart disease than men whose weight was satisfactory;

and the risk was nearly doubled for men with 20 per cent excess weight. The link between obesity and high risk of heart disease was also confirmed in the British Regional Heart Study and in the Scottish Heart Health Study. So there's certainly a link between obesity and heart disease, but it seems likely that it is the factors associated with being overweight (like becoming diabetic, having low levels of 'good' HDL cholesterol, high blood pressure, high triglycerides, and lack of exercise) that actually cause the damage, rather than the fact of being overweight on its own. In other words, research studies haven't found obesity to be an *independent* risk factor for heart disease. However, since obesity does indicate that a person is likely to be at increased risk of heart disease because of its association with other high-risk factors, and since it is a relatively easy danger sign to look for, its identification and treatment has an important place in any programme aimed at reducing coronary heart disease risk levels. A chart to check whether you are overweight can be found on page 81.

6 Stress

It is generally assumed that stress and overwork are linked to the likelihood of having a heart attack, but it is a difficult link to prove scientifically. One difficulty in this area concerns the problem of trying to define what we mean by 'stress'. A task that is seen as stressful by one person might be seen by another person as an enjoyable and rewarding challenge. Similarly, people in 'high-powered' jobs may have to make important policy decisions, but they will also frequently have the resources available to them for making and implementing such descisions, and this can result in the job being relatively non-stressful. On the other hand, those working under them, to whom many of the more difficult decisions about implementation will be passed, may have little or no control over the tasks assigned to them, will have fewer support services available to them, and will take home a lot less pay! It is quite likely, therefore, that they will suffer more strongly from stress-related ailments than their 'high-powered' bosses.

On a physical level, of course, it is quite possible to demonstrate how our bodies react to threatening, anxiety-provoking situations by the 'fight or flight' mechanism – and we can 'feel' it happening as we become geared up for the conflict. Our bodies produce more of the hormones adrenalin and noradrenalin in such situations, and the effect of this is to increase pulse rate and blood pressure, raise total cholesterol level, lower the 'good' HDL cholesterol, and increase the blood's tendency to clot. If such reactions occur too frequently or at too high a level of intensity in someone who already suffers from coronary heart disease, then they can help trigger off a heart attack; however, it is more difficult to prove that such stresses are direct causes of the arterial changes that occur in coronary heart disease.

Despite such difficulties, and some contradictory findings, there is a growing body of evidence to suggest that people who exhibit certain types of behaviour in stressful situations do tend to have an increased risk of developing heart disease. This particular be-haviour is often called 'Type A'. This applies to people who are aggressive, competitive, and have an exaggerated sense of 'time-urgency'. The most usual reactions to stress in the person prone to coronary heart disease are (according to the Type A theory) anger, hostility, and aggression. It also seems likely that it is the 'bottled-up' and 'simmering' anger/hostility that is more dangerous (to the person under stress) than the 'explosive, but temporary' kind of response – though the latter could be more dangerous to the casual bystander! Thus people who are subjected to consistently high levels of stress in circumstances over which they have little control, and who react with bottled-up anger, will be likely to suffer from some sort of physical or mental repercussions. Depression or excessive anxiety are common psychological responses to stress but it is quite probable that stress will also have certain physical consequences – and coronary heart disease may be one such consequence.

So although we need a certain amount of stress to keep us active and challenged in life, an excess can be harmful. It makes sense, therefore, to take advantage of the various techniques of stress management that are available. One such technique is the simple one of taking more exercise! It has been shown, for example, that exercise helps to reduce feelings of anxiety and depression and to promote feelings of 'well-being'. It also has the added bonus of reducing raised blood pressure levels and protecting against deterioration in the cardio-vascular system. A number of other stress-management techniques, such as relaxation exercises and the identification of coping strategies, also help – and these will be discussed more fully in Chapter 10.

7 Fibrinogen

The blood-clotting process is dependent on the interaction of a number of protein-clotting factors, one of which is fibrinogen. In fact, it is fibrinogen (together with something called Factor VII) that seems to be the key element in regulating this complicated process of clotting. However, when the levels of fibrinogen are too high, the blood tends to become 'sticky' and cannot flow easily through the blood vessels – thus leading to a greater risk of thrombosis.

As with two other substances in the blood, homocysteine and creatinine[1], there is still some debate as to whether a high level of fibrinogen is a direct risk factor in the development of heart disease, but it certainly has strong links with other risk factors such as obesity, high blood pressure, smoking, and raised cholesterol levels.

Fortunately, smokers are in a position to do something about raised fibrinogen levels, since stopping smoking will quickly reduce them. The level starts to fall immediately on stopping smoking, but it may take five years or more to reach the level of the non-smoker. Nevertheless, the damage can be undone, and the risk level reduced to the 'never-smoked' level in a few years. There is also evidence that the risk level can be reduced by engaging in vigorous exercise. This has been shown to reduce both raised fibrinogen levels and excess Factor VII activity (which is an even stronger predictor of sudden coronary death than raised fibrinogen or cholesterol).

8 Family history

There is a tendency for coronary heart disease and strokes to run in families, and heart disease developing in a close relative (e.g. a parent or brother/sister) under the age of 50 can be considered to be an important risk factor for other members of the family. This 'familial' risk element can be accounted for in part by the tendency of people in a family group to share similar lifestyles (including diet, drinking, and exercise habits), and effective measures (see Chapters 7 to 10) can be taken to modify these influences. Such measures will help to reduce the level of risk incurred as a result of hereditary factors.

We shall look more closely at the different types of familial hyperlipidaemias in Chapter 6, and in particular at the condition known as familial hypercholesterolaemia (FH), which is the most serious form of inherited illness involving raised blood fats, affecting roughly 1 in 500 people in Britain.

9 Diabetes

People with diabetes have a higher risk of developing heart disease than people without the condition. In diabetes, the body's ability to convert sugar from the foods we eat into energy is not functioning adequately, and the result of this defect is an excess of sugar in the blood. This leads to a reduction in energy levels and a compensatory search for other sources of energy. In particular, the body plunders its own reserve stores of fat and protein and this leads to one of the diagnostic symptoms of diabetes – loss of weight. The kidneys also excrete more water to try to get rid of the excess sugar and this produces two other common diabetic symptoms – frequency in passing urine and increased thirst.

There are two types of diabetes, insulin dependent diabetes and non-insulin dependent diabetes.[2] Unfortunately, both types of diabetes confer an added risk of heart disease.

In the Framingham Heart Study, the presence of diabetes doubled the risk of dying from heart disease, but the exact mechanism by which diabetes produces clogging of the arteries is not clear. It may be that it has something to do with the blood fat levels found in diabetics. Typically they will have raised triglycerides (as do sufferers from gout) and low HDL levels. Systolic blood pressure may also be raised. Whatever the precise link, it makes sense for people with diabetes to try to reduce their other risk factors where possible by paying especial attention to diet and exercise.

10 Gender

Evidence from the Framingham Heart Study shows clearly that, overall, men are about three times more likely to develop heart disease than women. However, the disparity in risk levels changes somewhat as we get older. Thus, women become more prone to develop coronary heart disease after the menopause, and by the time people have reached their mid-eighties, each sex has roughly the same risk of having a heart attack. It is likely that pre-menopausal women are protected in some way by the effects of the female hormone, oestrogen. From puberty until the menopause, women tend to have lower levels of total cholesterol and a lower risk of coronary heart disease than men[3]; but after the menopause (when their level of oestrogen falls off dramatically), women tend to have higher levels of total cholesterol, and their risk of developing heart disease increases.

Taking Hormone Replacement Therapy (HRT) substantially reduces the level of coronary heart disease for post-menopausal women, probably because of the effects of introducing a small dose of oestrogen.[4] Progesteron is also often added to reduce the risk of womb cancer, but this can tend to raise LDL cholesterol and so counteract to some extent the beneficial effects of oestrogen on total cholesterol levels.[5] Nevertheless, research has shown that the combined HRT still provides good protection against heart disease and offers even better protection against the development of osteoporosis (thinning of the bones) to which many older women are particularly prone and which can result in bone fractures.

As with the contraceptive pill, women using HRT may have a very slightly increased risk of developing blood clots in the veins (particularly in the early stages of treatment), but this has to be balanced against the positive advantages derived from the therapy. Apart from the protective effects against osteoporosis and heart disease there is also evidence, for example, that HRT may offer some protection against the development of Alzheimer's disease and help to reduce the incidence of death from breast cancer. The latter finding emerged from an American Cancer Society study of 400,000 post-menopausal women in which women taking HRT were shown to be 16 per cent less likely to die of breast cancer than non-users. Evidence from some other studies suggests, on the other hand, that prolonged use of HRT in post-menopausal women (over a period of five years or more) may lead to a small increase in the risk of developing this type of cancer. So at present the findings are not entirely clear-cut on this issue. There does seem to be some consensus that the risks of developing unwanted side-effects are small and that the benefits of taking HRT tend, in general, to outweigh the disadvantages. But since the circumstances will differ in each individual case, the best advice is that women contemplating the use of HRT should decide on the type and length of treatment after careful discussion with their GP.

As far as oral contraceptives are concerned, these also use combinations of oestrogen and a progesterone-type hormone called progestogen or, in the 'mini-pill', progestogen on its own. However, some of the early brands tended to have unwelcome side effects such as the tendency to raise blood pressure, increase the risk of a thrombosis, and sometimes increase cholesterol. With the advent of more sophisticated preparations, though, the risks of unwanted side effects have been much reduced, and some versions of the Pill may actually result in a rise in the 'good' HDL cholesterol levels which can help to reduce the risks. The decision on whether to use the Pill, or which Pill to use, is of course (like the decision about HRT) one that requires careful discussion with your GP.

11 Age

The chances of developing heart disease increase with age, and there is a much greater risk of developing the disease at age 65 or older than at age 30. This is probably because of the cumulative effect on the cardio-vascular system of such untreated risk factors as high blood pressure and raised levels of cholesterol. In other words, although the arteries have probably been furring up gradually for a long time, the effects of the damage only become evident from mid-life onwards when coronary heart disease strikes. However, a raised level of cholesterol at the age of 35 increases the risk of heart disease much more significantly than the same measurement at the age of 65. It is most beneficial, therefore, to detect and treat raised cholesterol levels earlier rather than later, in order to reduce risk levels later in life.

12 Country of origin

We have already seen that different countries have very different rates of coronary heart disease. In the Seven Countries Study, there was a very close relationship between raised average levels of cholesterol and incidence of heart disease, with Japan at the bottom of the scale and Finland at the top. In the wider 'nationality' league tables, Scotland and Northern Ireland come at the top of the league (with England and Wales roughly in line with Finland), and Japan is again at the bottom, with the lowest rates of heart disease, together with the Mediterranean countries such as France, Spain, Portugal, Italy, and Greece. So why do we get such regional variations in rates of coronary heart disease?

The answer lies partly in the different genetic make-up of people of different nationalities, with some groups having a greater vulnerability towards heart disease than others. In Britain, for example, people with a Celtic origin (the Scots and Irish) have a very high incidence of heart disease; Asians from the Indian subcontinent are particularly vulnerable to the development of diabetes (which of course carries an extra risk of heart disease); and

Afro-Caribbeans and Africans have a higher susceptibility to high blood pressure and strokes. However, these genetic factors aren't by any means the full story, since people who move from a country with a low-risk level (e.g. Japan) to a country higher up in the risk table (e.g. the USA) tend to have levels of risk that are closer to those of their adopted country than their country of origin. Similarly, Westerners moving to Japan tend to develop a lower risk profile. Therefore differences in levels of risk of heart disease can't be explained away by genetic factors alone – heredity deals the cards, as it were, but it is the environment that determines how they're played! And the most likely environmental factor at work in determining the way in which the cards are played is diet.

People in regions having a low coronary heart disease risk, such as the Mediterranean countries, tend to eat foods high in starch (like bread, pasta, and potatoes), high in monounsaturates, low in saturated fats, and they consume plenty of fish, fresh fruit, and vegetables. The diet in countries with a high incidence of heart disease, on the other hand, tends to favour processed foods with a high level of saturated fat, low fibre content, and a limited intake of fruit and vegetables. Thus, there seems to be a strong and consistent link between dietary factors and risk of heart disease, and since diet is something that we can modify without too much difficulty, it makes good sense to examine healthy eating approaches at some length (this we shall do in Chapters 7 and 8).

We can now summarize the position on risk factors. We have seen that it is possible to identify a number of independent risk factors, such as raised cholesterol and blood pressure, which increase the risk of heart disease on their own (i.e. after allowance has been made for other risk factors associated with them). There are also a number of other risk factors, such as obesity, that can help to identify people with an increased risk of heart disease, but probably don't by themselves directly cause the disease. We have noted that risk factors work by multiplying the chances of developing heart disease, so that whereas the possession of one risk factor may double your chance of developing heart disease, two will quadruple the risk, and three will produce an eightfold increase in your level of risk. On the other hand, we have also seen that it is possible to reduce our chances of developing the disease by introducing quite small changes to diet and lifestyle. Some practical suggestions about introducing such changes (where necessary) will be discussed in detail in Chapters 7 to 10, but before dealing with these issues we must return to the question of cholesterol. In the next three chapters we will look at the question of screening for raised cholesterol, at ways of assessing risk levels more precisely, and at different types of diseases involving raised blood fats.

4

Screening for raised cholesterol – who should be tested?

One of the difficulties with cholesterol is that it isn't usually possible to tell just by looking at someone whether they have raised levels or not! We might have a few clues, of course – their country of origin, lifestyle, diet – but what we can't see are the important 'hidden' variables, like the influence of heredity on a person's physical make-up. Thus the non-smoking female jogger with the healthy lifestyle might be predisposed to high cholesterol levels, whereas the man with a stressful, sedentary occupation who takes limited exercise, and is a heavy smoker, may turn out to have quite a low cholesterol reading. This 'smoking, couch-potato' is still a candidate for a coronary, though, despite his satisfactory cholesterol reading, since he has many other risk factors.

Since the only certain way of discovering whether people have cholesterol problems is to carry out a blood test, it could be argued that everyone should be offered a screening test – in the same way that we screen for diabetes or high blood pressure. Some doctors and health professionals do, indeed, suggest that everyone should be tested. Other doctors argue for opportunist screening, e.g. asking a person to have a cholesterol test only when they have come into the surgery for some other reason.[1] Yet another approach advocated by some doctors is what's called prioritized screening – which means screening those people who seem to be most at risk.

On balance, expert opinion tends to suggest that there are two main groups of people who should be the primary targets of screening, and we will now look at these groups. If you fall into either group, you should certainly press your GP or practice nurse to arrange a blood test for you.

First priority group

The first priority group consists of people in any of the following categories:

1 People under 65 who already have evidence of coronary heart disease.

2 People showing external signs of raised blood fats (i.e. hyper-lipidaemia).

In reference to the second category, there is sometimes evidence of cholesterol deposits on the body (especially in cases of familial hypercholesterolaemia (FH), one of the conditions to be discussed in Chapter 6). Yellowish lumps (called *xanthomas*) can appear on the tendons, especially the Achilles' tendon just above the heel, or on the tendons at the back of the hand. Cholesterol can also sometimes be detected in the eye as a whitish circle around the edge of the cornea (*corneal arcus*) or externally as small lumps on the thin skin at the corner of the eye (*xanthelasma*). These sorts of deposit in and around the eye are quite common in older people without FH, but they should be regarded as particularly significant if found in someone under the age of 50.

3 People with a family history of hyperlipidaemia.

4 People with a family history of premature death from heart disease in first-degree relatives (especially male relatives who have died before the age of 50, or female relatives who have died before 55).

5 People suffering from diabetes.

People in any of these above categories should certainly have their cholesterol checked. There is only one certain way of establishing your blood fat levels, and that is by sending off a sample of blood for analysis at the hospital laboratory. Even if you feel extremely healthy, do not suffer from high blood pressure, and live a healthy lifestyle (e.g. you take plenty of exercise and don't smoke), unfortunately this is no guarantee that you are immune to cholesterol problems resulting from an *inherited* tendency.

It is usually possible to modify general risk factors such as inactivity and smoking without seeking medical advice, but to deal adequately with certain inherited disorders, the person will need to seek proper medical help.

Second priority group

People in this group are those who have *two or more* of the following risk factors:

- raised blood pressure;
- smoking;
- inactivity;
- obesity.

As we have discussed earlier, it seems sensible in any prioritizing process to place men and post-menopausal women at the head of the queue, since they tend to have the highest total cholesterol levels. It is important, though, that we don't come to view cholesterol screening as something that we can safely leave until middle age, since the deposits that have formed in the arteries of people with cholesterol problems will have started to form at a much earlier age.

The fact is that the earlier cholesterol problems are identified, the greater the chance of avoiding damage to the cardio-vascular system in later years. So cholesterol screening should be seen as something that is clearly appropriate for the younger adult age group; and with people in the first priority group, it should be carried out at the earliest opportunity. Where total cholesterol is found to be 6.5 mmol/l or higher, or where the analysis shows clear abnormalities (e.g. raised triglycerides or low HDL), it is usually recommended that a re-test should take place after an interval of three months, and a further test three months after that. This period of time is needed in order to allow changes to diet or lifestyle an opportunity to take effect. With lower-risk groups, re-tests might be recommended after a period of six months or a year.

Cholesterol levels increase with age and are therefore lowest in children. So, as far as children of school age are concerned, it is generally not necessary to consider screening for cholesterol problems, apart from the children of people with a family history of raised cholesterol. Children who have a parent or sibling with known blood-fat abnormalities, or a parent with early-onset cardio-vascular disease, should be tested as a matter of course.

The need for post-test counselling

Whatever form of cholesterol testing is carried out, some form of follow-up advice is necessary, and the usual context in which this takes place is in a post-test discussion with the GP or practice nurse. Where the test takes place in the surgery, one would expect the necessary post-test counselling to take place more or less automatically. It is surprisingly easy, though, for busy GPs or nurses to forget how strong an impact the results of (to them) a routine blood test can have on a patient and often they underplay the need for personal counselling. Counselling needs to be tailored to the individual needs of the patient, and in some very severe cases of raised blood fats, such as FH (to be discussed in Chapter 6), more detailed advice will be required from a specialist hospital lipid clinic.

5

Measuring cholesterol and calculating risk scores

In the previous chapters, the phrase 'raised cholesterol level' has often been used, but we haven't defined exactly what constitutes a raised level of cholesterol. This is the question to which we will turn in the second half of this chapter, but first we must look at the methods used to measure cholesterol.

How to get your cholesterol measured

There are a number of ways to check your cholesterol, ranging from a test in the GP's surgery to using a cholesterol-testing kit in your own home. The main procedures used are: (1) venepuncture sample taken in the surgery and analysed in the local hospital laboratory; (2) finger-prick sample analysed in the surgery on a desk-top machine; and (3) finger-prick test using a cholesterol-testing kit obtained from the chemist and carried out at home.

1 Venepuncture sample taken in the surgery

The venepuncture test involves the GP or nurse taking a small sample of blood from the vein with a syringe. This sample is then sent off to the local hospital laboratory for analysis. Some surgeries carry this test out routinely as part of a 'Well Person' check, but other GPs may be reluctant to do the test routinely because of the expense.

Despite this variation in approach, most GPs will take a blood sample and send it off for analysis if you are persistent enough in asking for it, and particularly if you have reason to be concerned about your cholesterol level. If cholesterol testing is not offered as a routine service at your practice, you should certainly press to be tested if you fall into one of the two priority groups described in the previous chapter.

The analysis requested by your practice nurse/GP may in the first instance be for a measurement of total cholesterol level on its own, although a fuller 'blood lipid profile' – including measures of triglyceride and HDL – would be more informative, and give a better indication of risk level than the total cholesterol score alone. This should be performed following an overnight fast of 12 to 14 hours, and with no alcohol drunk for the previous 24 hours. The fasting test is particularly important if triglyceride is to be estimated and if LDL is to be calculated, since both these measurements are affected by recent intake of food and drink. After a few days, the results of the test will be returned to the surgery.

2 Finger-prick test analysed in the surgery by a desk-top machine

At some surgeries you might be offered a finger-prick test, which will give a total cholesterol measurement in a few minutes. (Some chemists may also provide this service.) In this test, a drop of blood is taken from your finger and the result analysed in a few minutes by a desk-top machine in the surgery. This sort of test will not offer a breakdown of cholesterol and triglyceride levels, but will provide an estimate of total cholesterol level.

3 Finger-prick test using a cholesterol-testing kit

It is now possible to buy a small cholesterol-testing kit over the counter in a chemist's shop. The test requires the person to obtain a drop of blood from the fingertip using a small device provided in the kit. The blood is massaged from the finger into the well of the small plastic test meter and left for a few minutes. The total cholesterol measurement can then be read off the measurement scale.

Some doctors are concerned that 'home testing kits' can provide misleading results as a consequence of what's called 'operator error' – the errors made by the person in carrying out the test (e.g. by not following the test instructions properly).

There is also sometimes a problem in knowing exactly how to interpret the results, despite the guidance notes that come with the kits. As one GP pointed out, 'There's a real danger of people getting hold of a figure and either being very worried about it (perhaps unnecessarily because they have no other risk factors) or being reassured about it when they do indeed have other risk factors.' This concern is certainly a real one, and it is undoubtedly best to have a cholesterol test carried out in the GP's surgery where adequate follow-up advice is available. However, the 'home testing kit' can be useful as a way of monitoring progress in between laboratory tests, and it may also offer a solution for those people who are frightened of going to their GP to have their cholesterol level checked. There is no doubt that where the test is done properly (and this is fairly easy to achieve provided the instructions are carefully followed and the initial finger prick is not done too tentatively), the results can be extremely accurate: 'My wife and I both did a finger-prick test within six hours of having a venepuncture sample taken. The results from the home testing kit and the hospital laboratory were very close indeed. My finger-prick test result was 5.01, and the laboratory measurement 5.1; and for my wife the scores were 3.80 and 3.9. We were very impressed.'

How accurate are cholesterol tests generally?

As with any test, there is always some uncertainty about how far the figure obtained represents an accurate estimate of the cholesterol level in that particular person's blood. Also, it has to be remembered that the level varies in the same person's blood from day to day, and even from hour to hour, depending on factors such as stress and type of food eaten.

However, the experience of people who have had their cholesterol tested repeatedly over long periods of time suggests that such wide variability would tend to be confined to particularly stressful episodes – either physically, psychologically, or both – or to periods in which they have begun to take medication or to make substantial changes to their diets. Otherwise, there is often a surprising consistency in the cholesterol readings obtained.

We have already seen that cholesterol and triglyceride levels can be affected by what we eat and drink, and they can also change according to biological factors. Thus cholesterol level tends to fluctuate in women according to the particular phase in the menstrual cycle, which is probably related to variations in oestrogen levels. Similarly, cholesterol tends to be raised during pregnancy, but this isn't related to coronary heart disease risk. There is also a tendency for total cholesterol and triglyeride to fall, and for the 'good' HDL to rise, during the summer months. These changes are most marked in countries where there are wide differences in temperatures between the seasons. So even in people with 'normal' levels of cholesterol, there could be a range of readings (even after fasting) taken at different times during the same year from 4 per cent to 12 per cent, and with triglycerides the range is even wider, from 14 per cent to over 40 per cent. The values also tend to be distorted in people recovering from an operation or illness, and it is usually recommended that any cholesterol test is delayed for about three weeks or so after flu, and three months after major surgery.

The cholesterol level tends to go down after surgery, and so an unrepresentative, low reading can sometimes result if taken too soon afterwards. This tendency is also found in readings taken shortly after a thrombosis in a coronary artery leading to heart muscle damage.

What these observations mean is that it is clearly unwise to rely on only one blood test in order to assess what we might call the 'prevailing' cholesterol level in a person; and a decision to prescribe medication should never be based on a single test.[1]

Apart from the problems of doing home testing accurately, even the best laboratories will have to allow for a 'margin of error' in their estimates of cholesterol levels in order to take account of the 'errors of measurement' that can affect all kinds of measuring processes. It has been estimated that in any particular lipid (blood-fat) analysis, the 'true' cholesterol score could lie anywhere between 3 per cent and 10 per cent of the actual score obtained on the test. Therefore it makes sense to concentrate on the trend of a number of scores rather than place too much credence on 'one-off' figures, and people with cholesterol problems will often need tests on a three-or six-monthly basis. Also, different laboratories may get slightly different results from one another, perhaps because they are using marginally different techniques.

Each of the measurement procedures (1) to (3) described above has a place in the process of checking cholesterol levels. In general, though, a full blood lipid profile obtained from a venepuncture sample under the supervision of the doctor or practice nurse is the most effective form of cholesterol testing. Whatever procedure is adopted, though, the important point is that it is used in a situation where some form of counselling is readily available (see Chapter 4), so that (in general) someone who uses a 'home testing kit' should still discuss the result with their GP or practice nurse.

What constitutes a raised cholesterol level?

To answer this question, we must first look at the way in which blood cholesterol levels are recorded, and we need to note that there are two methods of recording the level. In Britain, blood cholesterol is generally measured in millimoles per litre of plasma, plasma being the straw-coloured liquid in which the white and red blood cells and other substances are suspended.[2] The term is usually abbreviated to mmol/l. In the USA (and some other countries), the measurement of blood cholesterol is in milligrams per decilitre (mg/dl).[3] So a satisfactory level of cholesterol in Britain would be expressed as 5.2 mmol/l, whereas in the USA the same measurement would be expressed as 200 mg/dl (the higher the figure in each case, the higher the total cholesterol level).

As we have already seen, the risk of developing coronary heart disease rises with increasing total cholesterol levels, and most authorities suggest the following broad categories in relation to measures of cholesterol and level of risk:

Total cholesterol

less than 5.2 mmol/l (200mg/dl)   Desirable
(usually written as <5.2 mmol/l or <200 mg/dl)
Between 5.2 and 6.4 mmol/l (200–248 mg/dl)   Moderate risk
Between 6.5 and 7.8 mmol/l (250–300 mg/dl)   High risk
Greater than 7.8 mmol/l (300 mg/dl)   Very high risk
(usually written as >7.8 mmol/l or >300 mg/dl)

Compared with readings below 5.2 mmol/l, the risk of coronary thrombosis is roughly doubled when it reaches 6.5 mmol/l, trebled at 7.0 mmol/l, and quadrupled at 7.8 mmol/l and above. The UK has high rates of heart disease, and these are paralleled by similarly high levels of total cholesterol. As can be seen in Table 1, over two-thirds of the population are estimated to have total cholesterol levels in excess of the desirable 'target', i.e. they are 5.2 mmol/l or higher.

Table 1

Total cholesterol	Approx. percentage of UK population with this level	Risk of coronary heart disease
Below 5.2 mmol/l (200 mg/dl)	30%	Low
Between 5.2 and 6.4 mmol/l (200–248 mg/dl)	40%	Increasing risk
Between 6.5 and 7.8 mmol/l (250–300 mg/dl)	20%	Risk doubled
Above 7.8 mmol/l (>300 mg/dl)	10%	Risk quadrupled

As far as the identification of 'high risk' is concerned, most major 'cholesterol' studies have used the 6.5 mmol/l (250 mg/dl) cut-off point as the main criterion.

In drawing attention to risk levels it should be noted that they are not set in 'tablets of stone' (so you'll find different doctors may use slightly different cut-off points). Also cholesterol is only one of the heart disease risk factors which means that a high cholesterol score won't necessarily be linked to symptoms of heart disease, and a lower score won't make you immune to such problems. In fact, it has been estimated that approximately 50 per cent of coronaries occur in people with total cholesterol scores less than 6.5 mmol/l, and about a fifth can occur in people within the desirable range (below 5.2 mmol/l). As with other diseases, some people seem to have a stronger built-in protection to the development of coronary heart disease, despite having traits that in others would result in serious cardio-vascular problems. Nevertheless, it remains true that, in general terms, the higher the cholesterol score, the higher the risk of heart disease (particularly if linked to other risk factors), and the risk levels offer valuable guidelines for treatment.

If your test results only provide information about your total cholesterol score, then you will not need to refer to the tables that follow. These will be of interest, though, to those people who have had a full blood-fats profile, since they provide information about risk levels for HDL, LDL[4], and triglyceride scores, together with scores based on the ratio of HDL to LDL or total cholesterol. The risk levels for LDL and HDL cholesterol are set out in Table 2.

Table 2

LDL cholesterol[5]

Below 4.2 mmol/l (<162 mg/dl)	Desirable
Between 4.2 and 5.0 mmol/l (162–193 mg/dl)	Moderate risk
Above 5.0 mmol/l(>193 mg/dl)	Increasingly high risk

HDL cholesterol

Above 1.0 mmol/l (39 mg/dl)	Desirable
Between 0.9 and 1.0 mmol/l (35–39 mg/dl)	Moderate risk
Below 0.9 mmol/l (<35 mg/dl)	High risk in men
Below 1.1 mmol/l (<43 mg/dl)	High risk in women

Table 3 gives a guide to desirable levels of triglycerides.[6]

Table 3

Triglyceride

Below 2.0 mmol/l (<177 mg/dl)	Desirable
Between 2.0 and 4.5 mmol/l (177–400 mg/dl)	Some risk
Above 4.5 mmol/l (>400 mg/dl)	Increasingly high risk

Table 4 gives 'ratio' scores.

Table 4

Ratio measurements:
HDL ratio:
This is based on the formula: HDL cholesterol ÷ (total cholesterol –HDL).
The risk levels are:

Above 0.25	Desirable
Between 0.2 and 0.25	Moderate risk
Below 0.2	Increasingly high risk

So someone with a 'high-risk' total cholesterol score of 6.9 mmol/l, but a 'desirable' HDL level of 1.3, will have an HDL ratio of 1.3 ÷ (6.9–1.3) = 0.23; and this represents a 'moderate' level of risk overall. The ratio thus takes account of the 'protective' HDL element in calculating the overall risk level.

Total cholesterol/HDL ratio

This is calculated by dividing the total cholesterol figure by the HDL figure.

Above 5.0   Increasingly high risk

So if total cholesterol was a 'high risk' 7.7 mmol/l and HDL was a reasonable 1.2 mmol/l, the ratio would be 7.7 ÷ 1.2 = 6.4, in this case, still a high risk score even though allowance has been made for the 'protective' HDL element.[7]

LDL/HDL ratio

This less frequently used ratio is calculated by dividing LDL by HDL.[8]

Above 4.0   Increasingly high risk

Calculating risk scores: the Shaper score and the Dundee Coronary Risk Disk

Apart from risk levels based on cholesterol scores, there are other methods of calculating risk scores. One of these is the Shaper score and another the Dundee Coronary Risk Disk.

The Shaper score

Using data from the British Regional Heart Study, the Shaper scoring system aims to identify those people who have a high risk of suffering coronary heart disease. The score is obtained via answers to a set of questions. These questions are numerically weighted according to the degree of risk. As you will see, cholesterol level is not used as one of the factors in the risk calculation. This is not because cholesterol is considered unimportant, but that in this particular scoring system, aimed primarily at screening middle-aged British men (the majority of whom have raised cholesterol scores), cholesterol level on its own is not very useful. People within this age group, however, and especially those in the high-risk category, would certainly be advised to have their cholesterol checked. The way of working out the Shaper scoring system is set out below. You multiply the number of years spent smoking by 7.5, and then do the remaining calculations until a total figure is reached.

Number of years spent smoking × 7.5
> plus

systolic blood pressure (average of two readings) × 4.5
> plus

265 if person has been diagnosed as having coronary heart disease
> plus

150 if person currently suffers from angina
> plus

80 if one of parents has died of 'heart trouble'
> plus

150 if person suffers from diabetes

The scores are most relevant to men in the 40–59 age range, but scores are also given for 'high-risk' post-menopausal women. The scores indicating high risk are as follows:

Age group	Shaper score
Men aged 30–39	>800 (indicates they will be high risk by middle age)
Men aged 40–59	>1000
Men aged over 60	>1200
Post-menopausal women	>1200

Dundee Coronary Risk Disk

The Dundee Coronary Risk Disk[9] is a type of circular 'slide rule' calculator consisting of two rotating disks. The doctor or nurse enters values on to the front disk for each of the risk factors being considered (in this case, total cholesterol score, blood pressure, and smoking history), and then turns the Risk Disk over in order to read off the risk scores. These estimate the relative risk of the person having a coronary heart attack over a five-year period.

The calculation can be made using actual scores obtained for total cholesterol following a blood test, or by using one of the scores already provided as a representative figure for someone of that person's age and sex. It must be stressed, however, that the latter procedure only allows for the calculation of a very 'provisional' and rough estimate of risk. As far as blood pressure is concerned, the calculation requires either the systolic or the diastolic pressure, and in assessing smoking behaviour the scale allows for a variety of categories. It differentiates between cigarette and pipe or cigar smokers, and it also makes allowance for ex-smokers.

Case study DAVE

Dave is 49, single, and is a freelance book illustrator. He mostly eats a healthy, well-balanced diet, except for a tendency to eat rather a lot of cheese. He doesn't take much exercise, though, and smokes 20 cigarettes a day. He started smoking when he was 23, in his last year at art school, and he's smoked ever since. He discovered two years ago that he had raised cholesterol when he went for an insurance medical for a Permanent Health Protection Plan. He'd just gone freelance at the age of 47, and needed the insurance to provide financial cover in case he was unable to work because of illness. The same medical also revealed that he had what the doctor called problems with 'glucose metabolism'. Dave's father, who died after a heart attack in his mid-seventies, had suffered from 'maturity onset diabetes' from the age of 57, and the doctor thought that Dave might find the same problem starting to appear, although his blood glucose level wasn't yet high enough to diagnose him as a diabetic.

The tests showed that Dave's total cholesterol level was 6.4 mmol/l, with a low HDL level (0.70 mmol/l) and raised triglycerides (3.21 mmol/l). He was told that this sort of profile, with low HDL and raised triglyceride levels, was quite common in someone with problems of glucose metabolism. Although his total cholesterol score only put him at 'moderate risk' of developing coronary heart disease, he came into the 'high risk' category because of his low HDL level, linked with raised triglycerides, and a low HDL ratio of 0.12. He was also told that his smoking and high blood pressure (165/98) added substantially to his level of risk.

Needless to say, Dave wasn't too pleased with all this depressing news, since it meant he was going to have to pay an increased premium on his policy; but he was reassured by the GP's verdict that he should be able to reduce his risk level, and also reduce his glucose metabolism problems by paying close attention to his diet – cutting down on saturated fat and sweet foods – and by stopping smoking. The GP didn't promise any miracles, though, because the cholesterol profiles of people with 'diabetic-type' problems (especially the low HDL levels) tend to be difficult to correct. However, Dave thought it was worth a try.

The GP gave Dave a diet sheet and went through the various 'do's and don'ts'. He was quite surprised to find that Dave was already eating quite a low-fat diet – skimmed milk, plenty of fruit and vegetables, low-fat spreads and so on – but he told him that his high cheese consumption was one area where he could make further cuts in saturated fats. The GP also suggested that Dave should eat oily fish, like sardines and mackerel, at least three times a week. Dave thought this sounded a bit odd. What was the point of eating fatty fish when he was trying to *reduce* his fat intake? The doctor explained that the sort of oils provided by these fish were, in fact, extremely good for us, and for someone with Dave's high blood pressure, raised triglyceride, and low HDL levels, they were especially important. He also stressed the importance of soluble fibre in foods such as oats, fruit, vegetables, and pulses and as a non-meat eater, Dave was already familiar with these. The GP also suggested he should take a bit more exercise.

The first thing Dave did was to get his bike out of the shed. He'd promised himself he'd try the new cycle route into town sometime, and this gave him the spur he needed. The next decision he made was to cut down on his intake of cheese. He stuck to low-fat cottage cheese, apart from one small slice of low-fat hard cheese on Sundays, and made sure he got his daily dose of oats! He also made a determined effort to give up smoking. He'd been shocked when told how much his chances of developing a heart attack increased with smoking – as a smoker with raised blood pressure and high total cholesterol, he'd been told that he was eight times as likely to have a coronary as someone without these risk factors. And since diabetes (another risk factor) was 'waiting in the wings', as it were, he thought he'd better do something about the other three factors before it was too late!

By a determined effort, Dave managed to stop smoking altogether within a couple of months of his medical. 'It was the fear factor that did it – I was scared into giving it up!' He also kept to his new eating habits. His next test showed that his cholesterol had come down by leaps and bounds, followed a little more slowly by his blood pressure. He managed to get his cholesterol under 6 mmol/l within six months, and two years after his first blood test he'd amazed his GP by breaking the 5 mmol/l barrier with his new total cholesterol score of 4.8 mmol/l!

His HDL level was still rather low (0.82 mmol/l) and his triglyceride level slightly raised at 2.44 mmol/l. Both these levels were still unsatisfactory, but they related to his problem with glucose metabolism – and he knew he'd got a hard fight to keep them under control. However, as his doctor said, 'they're moving in the right direction' and his overall risk level had dropped dramatically. In particular, his improved HDL ratio (now 0.21 instead of 0.12) had moved him into the 'moderate risk' category instead of 'high risk'. Understandably, Dave was very proud of his success, felt much fitter than he had done for years, and was looking forward to surprising his GP even more in the future!

Dave's Dundee Risk Disk and Shaper scores

Dundee Coronary Risk Disk

After his insurance medical, Dave's GP calculated a risk score using the Dundee Coronary Risk Disk. This placed him in the group at 'most risk' of developing coronary heart disease.

After Dave had been on his low-fat diet for two years his GP calculated a further score which placed him in the 'inter-mediate risk' group, and much lower down the rank order in risk terms. The doctor was very pleased with his progress and told Dave that if he continued to remain a non-smoker for a further three years (i.e. five years in total) and assuming that his blood pressure (now 130/85) and total cholesterol remained the same, he would by then be moving into the 'least risk' group.

Shaper score

On the Shaper scoring system, Dave's initial score at the age of 47 (i.e. when he had his insurance medical) came out at 1003, calculated as follows:

number of years as a smoker $\times$ 7.5 = 24 $\times$ 7.5 = 180
  plus
systolic blood pressure $\times$ 4.5 = 165 $\times$ 4.5 = 743
  plus
the fact that his father had died of 'heart trouble' = 80

Total = 1003, which puts him in the high-risk category.

After two years his total score had dropped to 845, calculated as follows:

number of years as a smoker $\times$ 7.5 = 24 $\times$ 7.5 = 180
  plus
systolic blood pressure $\times$ 4.5 = 130 $\times$ 4.5 = 585
  plus
the fact that his father had died of 'heart trouble' = 80

Total score = 845, i.e. well under the 1,000 score needed to put a 49-year-old in the 'high risk' category.

6

Types of hyperlipidaemia

As mentioned earlier, hyperlipidaemia is the name given to the condition in which the blood fats (lipids) are raised to an extent that places the person at risk of coronary heart disease. So when total cholesterol, LDL cholesterol, or triglyceride measurements reach the sort of levels described in the previous chapter as 'high risk', we can say that someone has hyperlipidaemia.[1] It is also useful to distinguish between *primary* and *secondary* hyperlipidaemias – and since it is normal practice to exclude secondary hyperlipidaemia before calling the condition primary, we shall deal with the secondary factors first.

Secondary hyperlipidaemia

Having established that a person's blood-fats profile requires further investigation, the first step in the diagnosis of a hyperlipidaemic condition will usually involve the exclusion of possible secondary causes. Therefore your doctor might, for example, check for such factors as obesity or, at the other extreme, anorexia, both of which can result in blood-fat abnormalities, as can excess alcohol intake, which tends to raise triglycerides (as well as blood pressure). Hormonal influences during pregnancy produce a rise in cholesterol and triglyceride levels; and in women with primary hyperlipidaemia, the levels will need to be monitored very closely.

Similarly, checks might be made for hypothyroidism (underfunctioning of the thyroid gland) and for problems with liver and kidney functions. Tests for thyroid, renal, and liver function can be obtained routinely through the local hospital lab, and these will exclude hyperlipidaemia based on these factors. Blood glucose level will also reveal whether diabetes may be a cause for a distorted blood-fat profile (see page 17).

Primary hyperlipidaemia

Once secondary factors have been excluded, then it is reasonable to presume the presence of one of a number of primary hyperlipidaemias.[2] These are often related to some form of genetic abnormality, and it is important in such cases to see whether members of the immediate family are also affected.

The most severe form of primary hyperlipidaemia is the group of genetic disorders classified as *familial hyperlipidaemias*.

Familial hyperlipidaemias

Raised cholesterol can sometimes be produced by a number of independent genes clustering in an individual (when it is known as *polygenic hypercholesterolaemia*). In this form, which affects about 1 in 300 people, the range of total cholesterol levels tends to be between 6.5 and 9.0 mmol/l. Another form, which involves typical total cholesterol levels in the range 7.5 to 16.0 mmol/l or higher, is produced by a much clearer pattern of genetic transmission. This is the disorder known as *familial hypercholesterolaemia (FH)*, and it is estimated that this occurs in at least 1 in 500 individuals. There are two forms of FH. The most severe (and fortunately most rare) form, with a frequency of perhaps 1 in a million, is called *homozygous FH*, and in this the person inherits two defective genes, one from each parent. The more frequent form is called *heterozygous FH*, and in people with this disorder the defective gene is inherited from only one parent. The gene responsible for FH produces defective LDL receptors, and in consequence the cells fail to 'catch hold' of the LDL cholesterol as it moves around the body. This results in the accumulation of LDL cholesterol in the plasma, a rapid build-up of fatty deposits in the arteries, and the presence of 'external' cholesterol deposits, such as those that appear as hard yellowish lumps on the tendons of the hands or feet.

There are also some other forms of familial hyperlipidaemia. Some, such as *remnant particle disease*, are rare, but others – such as *familial combined hyperlipidaemia* (FCH) and *familial hypertriglyceridaemia* – are comparatively common.[3] Without treatment both lead to an increased risk of coronary heart disease and strokes.

Diagnosis of FH

At present, genetic testing in the UK is not particularly straightforward for FH. In general, therefore, the condition is usually diagnosed on the basis of a number of symptoms: in particular, people with FH have very high levels of LDL, and this is often accompanied by the physical signs of cholesterol deposits such as yellowish lumps on the tendons (*tendon xanthomas*), especially the Achilles' tendon above the heel. This may also be linked to recurring inflammation of the Achilles' tendon (*tendonitis*). Such lumps are also common on the hands, behind the knees, and on the elbows. Sometimes there is a whitish ring around the edge of the cornea in the eye (called a *corneal arcus*) – this is formed by deposits of cholesterol. Also, there may be yellowish lumps on the skin at the corner of the eye or on the eyelids (called *xanthelasma*). In addition to such physical signs, there will also be a history of hyperlipidaemia or coronary heart disease in the family.

With FH, it is essential that the condition is discovered as early as possible so that it can be treated – and thus prevent the consequent clogging of the arteries. It is also important that other members of the immediate family are tested, so that they can be treated if necessary. Even tests on young babies can reveal the condition.

The need for counselling

It is particularly important in cases of FH that adequate counselling is provided in the post-test setting to deal with what can be a very traumatic situation. It's not an easy task, of course, to find suitable ways of conveying information that is going to have a profound effect on people's lives. As one FH sufferer put it: 'Bad news is bad news, however it's delivered – but you can soften the blow by emphasizing that there is treatment.' 'Softening the blow' is particularly important at such times, and it's often helpful to draw attention to the fact that lots of people with FH live to a ripe old age despite their problems.

'I had two aunts who plainly had FH . . . they had rather unsightly cholesterol lumps . . . on their legs, . . . one died at 94 and the other at 89!'

Treatment for people with FH

In general, people with FH will require treatment by diet and medication. Dietary approaches are much the same as for people with more moderate cholesterol problems, and these will be covered in the next chapter. In dealing with FH schoolchildren, however, the school must be made to realize that this is a serious genetic problem, and that the dietary requirements in school meals must be taken seriously.

Medication is aimed at correcting the high LDL levels, and this will be discussed in Chapter 11, together with certain other specialized techniques that are used in those cases of FH that do not respond adequately to medication and diet. The question of gene therapy is one that has to be left to future research, but there is no doubt that FH would offer an exciting area for such therapy given the development of suitably sophisticated methods of diagnosis and intervention.

FH and having children

This sufferer of FH articulates the dilemma for potential parents very clearly: 'There's the problem of whether you should have children if you know you've got this defect, now that we know it exists as a single gene defect. It is a moral dilemma.'

For many people with FH, of course, this dilemma has not caused any difficulty, since they were unaware that they were suffering from FH when they decided to have children. If they *are* aware, though, it is important to consider the position. If only one of the parents has FH there's a 50/50 chance that the child will develop heterozygous FH – but this form of the disease can be treated successfully. For the most part, the problems arise where *both* parents suffer from FH. If these parents have four children, the chances are that one will be normal, two will have heterozygous FH, and one will have the more difficult to treat, homozygous FH.

Fortunately, the chances of two people with FH marrying is not particularly high. It is also encouraging to know that FH does not skip a generation and then reappear. So if a person doesn't have FH (even if other members of the family do have the condition), he or she cannot pass it on to the children or to future generations. The fact that a diagnosis of FH can be made without too much difficulty (it's even possible sometimes for the diagnosis to be made at birth in 'at risk' babies by measuring LDL levels in blood taken from the umbilical cord) also offers the hope that the major damaging effects of the disorder can be prevented to a large extent. What is required is a greater degree of public awareness of the potential problems associated with raised cholesterol, and a better take-up of the screening procedures described in Chapter 4. This will result in more effective identification of the people at risk and, once diagnosed, the FH can be treated.

The next five chapters examine a variety of approaches to treating raised cholesterol levels . In Chapters 7 to 10 we look at the effects of diet, exercise, and other lifestyle changes in lowering cholesterol, and then in Chapter 11 we shall consider the use of medication and other forms of treatment.

Case Study ANNE

Anne is 32 and works as a part-time cleaner at a local nursing home. Her husband, Steve, works for a firm of builders, and they have two school-aged children – Darren (14) and Tracy (12). Anne had noticed that she had some hard yellowish lumps at the back of her ankles above her heels, together with a couple of small lumps on the back of her hands. She'd had them for years, but she thought they were just hard pieces of skin. Her father, who died five years ago at the age of 45 from a severe heart attack, had similar lumps, as did one of his younger sisters. Anne thought her lumps were a bit unsightly, but because they weren't any bother she regarded them simply as some sort of harmless family quirk!

Then about three years ago Anne went for a routine eye test and the optician remarked on the fact that she had a white ring around the coloured part of the eye called a corneal arcus. He explained that this white ring could sometimes indicate raised cholesterol levels, and referred Anne to her GP to have it checked out. The test revealed a very high total cholesterol level (13.6 mmol/l), and Anne was referred to a hospital consultant.

After further tests at the hospital, including another blood test and an ECG (which tests the functioning of the heart), the consultant confirmed that Anne was suffering from familial hypercholesterolaemia (FH). She explained the nature of the disease, how it affected the blood vessels and the heart (hence, the reason for having an ECG), and how the lumps on her hands and ankles and the white ring in her eye were the result of cholesterol deposits. She also told Anne how it is possible to treat the condition by diet, or diet combined with medication. An appointment was made for Anne to see the dietitian, who explained the need to cut down on saturated fats and gave her advice on modifying her diet. At a later stage, Anne was also put on the drug simvastatin, which helped to control her cholesterol level.

At her first visit to the consultant, Anne was also asked to give a full family history, which revealed that quite a few of the relatives on her father's side had died at an early age from heart disease. The consultant was keen to arrange for Anne's family to have blood tests, particularly Darren and Tracy; and she advised that other relatives on her father's side who hadn't had their cholesterol checked should have it tested. She explained that FH was an inherited disease that could affect her own children and other relatives of her father. She felt it was safe to assume that Anne had inherited FH from her father because of his medical history, the presence of yellowish lumps on his hands and ankles, and the fact that his widow was unaffected – she'd already had her cholesterol checked at a 'Well Person' clinic. However, the consultant pointed out that the only way of telling which relatives had inherited the defective gene was by checking the level of cholesterol in the blood.

The consultant then arranged to see the whole family and discussed the question of blood tests with them. Steve was very reluctant to take part at first, since there didn't seem to be any problem on his side of the family – but Darren would only agree if his Dad went along as well! Apart from Darren's blackmail, what finally convinced Steve that it was worth having the test done was the doctor's comment that the only effective way in which you can identify whether you have a cholesterol problem is by having a blood test. She explained that people with severe cholesterol problems are often quite unaware of the damage occurring in their arteries until they begin to suffer the consequences of coronary heart disease. She also told him that you can still have cholesterol problems even if other members of the family don't appear to have them, since there are other types of cholesterol problems apart from FH. Steve wasn't too keen on this piece of information, but he was reassured by her comment that if you do turn out to have a problem, it can usually be treated successfully – and the earlier you can identify it, the greater the chances of success. So the tests were duly arranged.

The whole family was on tenterhooks waiting for the results. When they finally came through, Steve was relieved to hear that although his cholesterol was a bit raised (6.3 mmol/l), it didn't reach the levels indicative of FH. He was advised, though, to reduce his intake of saturated fat, to stop smoking, and to have another test in six months' time. Tracy's cholesterol level was a healthy 3.9 mmol/l, but unfortunately Darren, like his mother, had a very high cholesterol level (11.2 mmol/l). The defective gene appeared to have passed down to Darren and he would need treatment for FH. Needless to say, he was a bit fed up with the idea of having to change his diet and possibly take tablets, but he started to take a keen interest in some of his mum's new low-fat recipes (which he had to admit he enjoyed as much, and sometimes more, than the old ones). And although at first he thought he'd have preferred not to have known about FH, he's now pleased that he does. The fact that his condition has been identified at this early age means that there is a good chance of keeping his cholesterol level under control and of preventing the rapid development of atherosclerosis and its associated problems.

7

Lowering cholesterol by diet (1): fats and fibre

The good news in the cholesterol story is that raised fat levels in the blood can often be controlled by diet and lifestyle changes alone, and it is these essential aspects of treatment that we shall look at in the next four chapters. In this chapter we shall examine the effects of fats and fibre on cholesterol levels and in Chapter 8 we will look at the role of drinks, food supplements, and special diets. Then in Chapters 9 and 10 we shall discuss the importance of exercise and other lifestyle changes. To begin with, though, we shall look at the role that diet has to play in dealing with cholesterol problems.

Are dietary changes effective in keeping cholesterol in check?

You may have come across the occasional newspaper report (or even sometimes a sceptical remark from a medical practitioner) claiming that modification to diet is only minimally effective as a means of lowering cholesterol. However, this view does not reflect the facts, and is counterbalanced by the more experienced judgements of consultants and dietitians working in this field. They routinely report reductions in total cholesterol levels of between 15 per cent to 30 per cent (and often very much higher) in patients following their dietary advice.

So it's abundantly clear that diet *does* play a crucial role in the treatment of raised cholesterol – however many contrary opinions you may come across! The evidence is indisputable (and extremely encouraging) on this point.

The extent of the changes that can be achieved can be seen in the reduction in average cholesterol levels that have been attained in some countries (such as Australia and the USA) as a result of national health education programmes – and even small reductions in cholesterol levels can result in major health benefits. You may recall that a reduction of 0.6 mmol/l in total cholesterol level (a reduction easily achievable by dietary means) can reduce the risk of coronary heart disease by up to 50 per cent. It has been estimated that a 35-year-old man who reduced his cholesterol level by this amount would be halving his risk of developing heart disease by the age of 40 – and even people over 70 can reduce their risk by 20 per cent!

Some personal experiences

This small selection of personal experiences illustrates the remarkable successes that can be achieved by people who are dealing with cholesterol problems by dietary means:

- 'In six months on a low-fat diet, I got my total cholesterol level down from 6.0 mmol/l to 4.4.'
- 'I got my cholesterol down from 6.7 to 4.0 in six weeks on a diet, just to show I could do it. Then I took a rather laid back attitude, and it went back up to 6.4!'
- 'They found very raised figures for cholesterol – 8.4. On a re-test it went down to 7.8, and six months later – after going on a diet and using a cholesterol-lowering margarine – my cholesterol had gone down to 5.4.'

Experiences of this sort are common, and they show how someone can make excellent progress in lowering levels of total cholesterol provided a serious attempt is made to stick to the type of dietary advice described in this chapter and the following one. Such diets need not be boring or unexciting, as can be seen from the recipes in Chapter 13. A good dietary principle for people dealing with cholesterol problems is to include as much variety as possible in the type of food consumed, while at the same time keeping to general cholesterol-lowering guidelines. So to find out what type of foods are good for keeping cholesterol in check, we will look first of all at the role of fats and fibre.

The role of fats

We have already seen that dietary cholesterol (the sort contained in egg yolk, meat and some shellfish) is not the most important contributor to the level of cholesterol in the blood; this distinction is reserved for the fats and oils in our food. By far the greatest proportion of the body's cholesterol is manufactured in the liver from substances that are derived from the various fats and oils that are present in food, either in observable form (as in butter, margarine, or cooking oil), or in disguised forms such as the fat

46

contained in biscuits or cakes. So it is the type and amount of fats and oils present in our diet that we need to look at most closely in the fight against raised cholesterol.

The main difference between fats and oils is that fats are solid or semi-solid at room temperature, whereas oils are liquid; but they are essentially similar in that both consist of what are called fatty acids. There are many different fatty acids, but they can be grouped into one of three main types according to their chemical structure. These types are *saturates*, *polyunsaturates* and *monounsaturates* (the latter two both being unsaturated fats), and it is the effects that each of these fatty acids has on cholesterol levels that we shall need to examine particularly closely in this chapter. It is important to appreciate, however, that the different fats and oils found in food are invariably a combination of different fatty acids. So even butter, which is usually described as a 'saturated fat' (and does have a concentration of over two-thirds saturated fat), also has quite a high proportion of monounsaturates in it (around a quarter of the fat); and you might find that a margarine labelled 'high in polyunsaturates' (which probably indicates over 50 per cent polyunsaturated fat) also has quite high amounts of saturates and monounsaturates (making up the remaining fat content in roughly equal proportions). Similarly, a 'monounsaturated' oil such as olive oil, which has over 70 per cent monounsaturates, will also contain 12–14 per cent each of polyunsaturates and saturates (see Figure 1 overleaf). You can find out the exact amounts of different types of fat by looking at the nutritional information on the product.

Saturates

Since all fats contain a mixture of different sorts of fatty acids, it is the balance of the various types of fatty acid in the food we eat that becomes important in the context of cholesterol. In particular, we know that it is the *saturated fats* (the ones that are solid or semi-solid at room temperature) that tend to be most active in raising cholesterol levels, whereas the unsaturated fatty acids (the monounsaturates and polyunsaturates) tend to have the effect of lowering total cholesterol levels. A main dietary aim for people with cholesterol problems, therefore, is to keep saturated fats at a low level. But how do we know how much of the fat contained in various foods is saturated? The answer is that you need to check the nutritional information on food labels. You will find that in most of the larger supermarkets, the percentage of saturated, polyun-

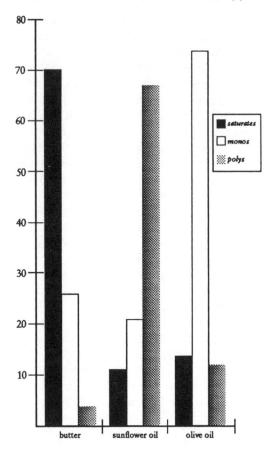

Figure 1 Relative proportions of saturated and unsaturated fatty acids in butter, sunflower oil, and olive oil

saturated, and monounsaturated fats in the product is listed on the nutritional label.

Checking the actual percentage of fats in the products you buy is the only sure way of knowing how much saturated fat they contain, but there are some general guidelines. We know, for example, that saturated fats are predominantly found in foods of animal origin such as:

- fatty meats and meat products such as sausages, fatty mince, and meat pies;

48

- whole cream milk (as opposed to skimmed);
- creamy yoghurts (e.g. Greek-style yoghurts);
- hard cheese and full fat soft cheese;
- butter, hard margarines, lard, suet.

High concentrations are also found in:

- palm oil and coconut oil;
- many cakes, biscuits, ice creams, and chocolates.

If this list happens to contain all your favourite treats, don't despair! As you read on (and do your own investigations by studying the small print in the supermarket), you will find that there is a whole range of similar products that are made with very low levels of saturated fat. You should certainly be able to find a good variety of nutritious and tasty food that has a saturated fat content of five to ten per cent or less. If you look out for labels such as 'low fat', 'low in saturates' and 'half fat', and then check the percentage of saturated fat (such checks are necessary because the manufacturer's idea of 'low fat' might not coincide with your view), you will find that even some brands of ice-cream are acceptable in a cholesterol-lowering diet!

Polyunsaturates

Because saturated fats tend to raise cholesterol levels, the two unsaturated fatty acids, polyunsaturates and monounsaturates, are generally preferred choices for people with cholesterol problems. We will discuss later the recommendations as to the balance of unsaturates to saturates in a healthy cholesterol-lowering diet, but first we will examine the nature of the two unsaturated fatty acids, beginning with the polyunsaturates. A good concentration of the polyunsaturated fatty acids is found in:

- sunflower, safflower, corn and soya bean oil;
- many nuts, especially walnuts, pine nuts and sunflower seeds (brazil nuts are similarly high in polunsaturates and monounsaturates – but also include 16 per cent saturates);
- oily fish such as mackerel, salmon, herring, sardine, pilchards, trout and tuna.

These fatty acids generally remain liquid both at room temperature and also when refrigerated (unlike monounsaturates, which tend to become semi-solid in the fridge). Some polyunsaturated fatty acids can be made by our bodies, but others can only be obtained satisfactorily by ensuring an adequate intake from our diet. These are called the *essential fatty acids* (*omega-6* and *omega-3*), and for a healthy diet it is essential that we obtain a sufficient supply of these fatty acids.

The omega-6 fatty acids are mainly derived from *linoleic acid*, which in turn is obtained from vegetable oils such as sunflower seed oil. So it is important that we have an adequate intake of linoleic acid from such dietary sources, and this general nutritional advice has added importance for people with raised cholesterol, since omega-6 fatty acids actually help to lower cholesterol levels.

The omega-3 fatty acids, on the other hand, are derived primarily from *linolenic acid*, and found in some vegetable oils such as soya bean and rapeseed oil, oily fish such as mackerel, herring, salmon and sardine, and in eggs from hens fed on omega-3 rich diets. Our bodies only need a small quantity of omega-3 fatty acids, and a normal, balanced diet will supply these. For people with cholesterol problems, however, the two fatty acids obtained from oily fish are particularly beneficial. These are usually referred to as EPA and DHA,[1] and can play a very important role in keeping cholesterol problems in check. Unlike omega-6 fatty acids, the omega-3 variety aren't particularly effective in reducing LDL cholesterol, but there is evidence to suggest that they can help to raise HDL levels. They are very effective in lowering triglycerides, in reducing fibrinogen levels (thus inhibiting the formation of blood clots), and they may also be of value in the control of high blood pressure. All these features offer protection against coronary heart disease, and it is perhaps not surprising therefore that people from fish-eating countries, such as the Eskimos and Japanese, have very low rates of heart disease, and that fish eaters generally tend to live longer than non-fish eaters!

Taking capsules of fish oil supplement, however, is much less effective than eating the actual fish itself. It has been demonstrated, for example, that eating two or three portions of oily fish each week can reduce levels of triglycerides significantly, but to obtain the same level of omega-3 from capsules would require a very large capsule intake indeed! As can be seen from Table 1, smoked mackerel is a particularly rich source of omega-3 (though for people who need to be careful about dietary cholesterol, it should be pointed out that the smoked version of mackerel does include quite a high cholesterol content). The only difference between smoked and ordinary mackerel is that the smoked variety has less water content, and so contains a slightly higher concentration of omega-3 per 100 g. Sardines, whether fresh or tinned, also provide a good source, but tuna needs to be eaten fresh or frozen to provide the same benefit, since the cooking process that precedes the tinning of tuna removes most of the omega-3 content. The most cost-effective form of dietary supplement would be one or two teaspoons of cod liver oil a day (rather than capsules).

Table 1 Omega-3 content of fish oil from various sources

Sources of fish oil

Smoked mackerel 100 g	3.5 g
Poached salmon 100 g	2.7 g
Herring 100 g	1.8 g
Sardine 100 g	1.5 g
Spratt 100 g	1.5 g
Pilchards (canned)	1.4 g
Cod liver oil 1 tsp	0.85 g
Trout (rainbow) 100 g	0.5 g
Scampi (fried) 100 g	0.5 g
Tuna (canned in oil) 100 g	0.3 g
Cod (steamed) 100 g	0.3 g
Haddock (steamed) 100 g	0.3 g
Cod liver oil capsule	0.05 g
Halibut oil capsule	0.03 g

Monounsaturates

Several foods are high in *monounsaturates*, including:

- olive, groundnut (peanut) and rapeseed oil;
- many nuts, especially hazelnuts, almonds, pecan nuts and peanuts;
- avocados and olives.

The replacement of some of the saturated fat in our diet by monounsaturates is a particularly beneficial change, since it tends to lower the 'bad' LDL cholesterol, but doesn't at the same time decrease the 'good' HDL levels. In fact, there is some evidence that monounsaturates may sometimes help to increase HDL cholesterol. Remember, though, that if eaten too liberally, the high-fat/high-calorific value of some monounsaturated foods, e.g. avocado, nuts, and olives (also high in salt because they are bottled in brine), will tend to increase your weight! In its ability to lower LDL cholesterol without reducing HDL levels, the monounsaturated fatty acid has a slight advantage over the polyunsaturates which, if consumed in large amounts as saturate replacements, tend to reduce the 'good' HDL. In general, though, the amounts of polyunsaturated fats eaten in a balanced diet aimed at reducing total cholesterol level should not produce this effect.

The fact that monounsaturates have such an excellent record in helping to keep LDL cholesterol in check without reducing levels of HDL (and in some cases even increasing them), has led to a greater interest in the use of monounsaturated oils in cooking, and we shall look at this aspect of the 'fat story' in the next chapter in the section on the Mediterranean diet.

Spreading fats – butter versus margarine

The highest concentration of saturated fatty acids, as we have seen, is in butter (more than two-thirds of the fat is saturated), and its total fat content is over 80 per cent.[2] Also, unlike margarine and oils, butter contains quite a lot of dietary cholesterol, which is another disadvantage for people with severe cholesterol problems. Therefore, for those individuals with raised blood-fat levels, this probably means avoiding butter altogether, or keeping it for special treats and instead using the low-fat spreads that are now on the market – some have a total fat content of under 20 per cent, and a saturated fat percentage of well under 5 per cent.

On the other hand, these margarines are not entirely free from problems either! The low-fat spreads are certainly much lower in saturates than butter, but most solid or semi-solid forms of fat made from vegetable oil contain certain fatty acids (called *trans-fatty acids*) that are treated by the body like saturates. These trans-fatty acids are produced as a result of a process known as *hydrogenation*[3] that is used to convert unsaturated vegetable oils into solid fat suitable for use in baking and for spreading. So you will find that hydrogenated or partially hydrogenated fats are used widely in the production of margarines, biscuits, pastries and cakes.[4] (Trans-fatty acids also occur naturally in some animal fats, and butter contains about 5–6 per cent.) Unfortunately, eating lots of foods containing trans-fatty acids tends to increase LDL and lower the 'good' HDL cholesterol levels, increasing the risk of heart disease. A daily intake below 5 grams is usually advised, and using one of the many spreads with less than 1 per cent hydrogenated fat, or with none, e.g. one thickened with guar gum, can help in achieving this target.

The best advice then is to choose a low-fat, low-saturates, low trans-fatty acid spread and use it sparingly! You may, though, be a little less sparing in the use of low-fat spreads (or foods) fortified with *plant stanols* or *sterols.* Although only a small proportion of these plant extracts is absorbed by the body they have the effect of displacing cholesterol in the gut; and the use of such fortified spreads two or three times a day can produce a significant reduction in the body's uptake of LDL cholesterol without lowering HDL.

Cooking fats

With cooking fats, apart from butter (which we have already discussed), the highest fat (and saturated fat) content is in the products made from animal fats – lard, dripping, and suet. The total fat content is often approaching 100 per cent, with saturated fat levels around 40–55 per cent (as in beef dripping). Animal cooking fats may also have quite high concentrations of dietary cholesterol. Low-fat margarines would be a better bet (apart from the problems associated with hydrogenation) but unfortunately the low-fat spreads with least saturated fat tend not to be suitable for use in cooking (or for freezing). So the best approach for people on a cholesterol-lowering diet is to avoid cooking in fat. Grill, poach, or microwave where this is a suitable alternative, or use the mono-unsaturated or polyunsaturated oils.

Fats in meat and cheese

Meat

The frequently heard view that you should cut out red meat on a cholesterol-lowering diet is not based on an accurate interpretation of the evidence. It is true that fatty cuts of red meat will tend to be high in saturates and will include some dietary cholesterol. But lean cuts can have a relatively low saturated fat content, and dietary cholesterol isn't usually a major concern, so it's certainly not essential to deprive yourself of red meat if you are particularly fond of it. For example, lean beef is quite low in fat (often under five per cent), with an average saturated fat content of under two per cent. Some cuts of red meat, on the other hand, are extremely fatty (e.g. lamb chops), so the advice generally would be to choose lean cuts or to trim off the fat. As far as white meats are concerned, such as chicken and turkey, these have quite a low saturated fat content generally – but you'll still need to be wary of the rich, creamy sauces that often accompany them! With other meats, you just have to check the fat levels of the various cuts. A lean, loin pork chop that has been grilled is likely to be around 10 per cent total fat, for example, of which about a third is likely to be saturated fat. The fat content of bacon, on the other hand, tends to be high (both in total and saturated levels).

With ham, you're on a better wicket, since lean ham is a low-fat product (often around 5 per cent total fat). Be careful about chopped ham in tins, though, and 'Spam', which can be quite high in fat (often around 25 per cent or more in total fat content). Similarly, sausages, meat pies, and mince frequently contain a high level of saturated fat. So make sure you choose those products labelled 'low fat', and then grill rather than fry. This way, you should be able to keep the fat levels within reasonable limits.

Cheese

As far as cheese is concerned, most of the traditional brands of hard cheese, together with the full-fat soft cheeses, tend to be very high in saturates (averaging around 20 per cent). Standard cheddar cheese is about one-third fat, with over 20 per cent saturated; and cream cheese is nearly 50 per cent fat, with 30 per cent saturated.

As with other foods containing a high saturated fat content, it is possible to find alternative cheese products with acceptable levels of fat. Low- or half-fat cottage cheese, for example, is usually very low in saturated fat content (usually around two per cent or less), low-fat fromage frais is usually under three per cent saturated, and sometimes available in a 'virtually fat-free' variety with less than 0.1 per cent total fat content. It is also now possible to buy varieties of hard cheese with a very much reduced percentage of saturates.

Hidden fats

So far we have discussed types of fat in foods that we tend to think of as containing fat, like margarine, cooking oils, and oily fish. We must now look at those foods that contain fat in *hidden* forms.

Biscuits

A typical chocolate digestive biscuit might contain around 25 per cent total fat, over half of which is saturated fat; and a shortbread biscuit might contain an even higher proportion of saturates. An oatbran crispbread, on the other hand, can have less than three per cent total fat, with under one per cent saturated.

Cakes and pastries

Cakes and pastries are often thought of as a 'no-go' area, but in fact, from a cholesterol-lowering viewpoint, it's only cakes and pastries with a high saturated fat content that need to be avoided; and, in the case of people with raised triglyceride levels, high sugar levels. Unfortunately, many of the cakes and pastries that we buy are baked with fats high in saturates. Cakes and pastries can quite easily be made with monounsaturates or polyunsaturates, however, and the taste is every bit as good as the saturated variety. You can test out this assertion by trying one of my recipes for cakes made with olive oil (see Chapter 13). For people on very strict cholesterol diets that include the restriction of dietary cholesterol, there are also some excellent egg-free cake recipes included in the same chapter. In fact, all that is usually necessary to make very tasty 'egg-free' cakes and buns is to substitute in any standard recipe two tablespoonfuls of milk for each egg; and remember that egg whites are cholesterol-free. So, for example, meringues or macaroons are fine, provided you don't need to restrict your intake of sugar.

Crisps

Crisps are not bad for you if eaten in moderation. Again, it depends on the amount and type of fat involved, and this can only be determined by examining the side of the crisp packet. It's true that the standard packet of crisps does tend to have quite a high fat content, often over 30 per cent in total, with a saturated fat content around ten per cent, but you will also find that the major fat constituents in a lot of crisps are, in fact, monounsaturates and polyunsaturates. So if you're keen on an occasional packet of crisps (say once a week or so), it's worth doing your own 'fat content' survey to hunt out the tastiest low-fat, low-saturates varieties that are also free from hydrogenated fat. If you're trying to lose weight, you need to remember that crisps are high in calories, so the emphasis should be on the word 'occasional' (i.e. in this case, rather less than once a week)!

Chocolate

Chocolates tend to be rather high in fat, and the saturated fat component can be quite substantial. However, they also vary considerably, and by inspecting the label you might find a chocolate bar with a reduced fat content (say, under 20 per cent fat and less than ten per cent saturates). Moreover, the fat in a lot of chocolate is derived from cocoa-butter which consists of stearic acid and this saturated fatty acid is converted in the body to monounsaturated fat. This means that products containing cocoa-butter are likely to be less harmful as cholesterol raising agents than those containing other saturated fatty acids. (Incidentally, chocolate is also quite high in flavonoids (see page 68) which have beneficial anti-oxidant properties.) Unfortunately a lot of chocolates contain *large* amounts of cocoa-butter and some also contain quite a lot of other fats, such as highly saturated milk fat. And the mixture of cocoa-butter with other fats can then result in a final product which once again becomes a cholesterol-raiser!

On the whole, you will probably find that you have a better chance of finding a low-fat, sweet treat with non-chocolate confectionery! Boiled sweets, fruit gums, pastilles, peppermints, and liquorice allsorts, for example, are all between 0 per cent and 2.2 per cent total fat, and the saturated element is negligible (all less than one per cent). The downside is that they are rather high in sugar, and hence they're bad news for the slimmer, those with raised triglycerides, and those who wish to keep their teeth!

Relating food intake to energy output

Food provides the necessary fuel for our bodies to work properly, thus our energy is derived from the fats, carbohydrates and protein contained in the food we eat (and also in the liquids we drink, especially alcohol). Unfortunately, many of us tend to take in much more body fuel (food) than our energy output requires, with the result that we put on weight.

Measuring energy requirements

The way in which energy values are measured is by *calories*. One calorie represents the energy required to raise one kilogram of water from 15°C to 16°C. If you look at the nutritional labels found on food items, you will find that energy levels are referred to as *kilocalories (kcal)* – these are the calorie values. You will also usually find another energy value on the label referred to as a *kilojoule (kJ)*, and this is simply a metric equivalent of the calorie. Most adults need about 2,000–2,500 calories (or 8,000–10,000 kilojoules) a day in order to function properly.

Fats

Foods containing fats are the most concentrated supply of energy-providing food, and they will quickly become stored as body fat if excess amounts are eaten – either in dairy produce, cooking fats/oils, and spreads, or in a 'hidden' form – as in biscuits and cakes. One typical chocolate biscuit, for example, might have something like 30 per cent fat, and contain nearly 100 calories – and you'd have to do at least one hour of jogging to use up the energy supplied by just three chocolate biscuits! So beware of the hidden-fat foods and concentrate instead on carbohydrates.

Carbohydrates

These can be divided into those that are 'available' to provide energy[5] (and are contained in most sweet foods and starches), and those contained in foods of plant origin such as cereals, pulses, fruits, and vegetables, which are 'unavailable' for energy purposes, but play a vital role as dietary fibre. Starches, or complex carbohydrates as they have come to be known, are a particularly good substitute for fat. Foods particularly high in complex carbohydrates include:

- bread;

- potatoes;
- rice and pasta.

These should form a substantial part of a healthy (and slimming) diet.

Protein

Protein is important for growth and repair of body tissues, and tends to be used as a 'third-string' energy provider to fats and carbohydrates. It is readily available in:

- milk and other dairy products;
- fish and meat;

but it is also found in a wide range of other foods such as:

- bread;
- potatoes;
- cereals;
- nuts, beans, and pulses.

So the 10–15 per cent of calories we need to get from protein is not difficult to obtain on a well-balanced diet.

How much fat do we need?

When it comes to recommendations about the proportion of our energy needs that should be provided by fats in our diet, the best current advice is that this should be not more than 30–35 per cent (for some people on strict lipid-lowering diets, it may be a bit less); and of this it is preferable to aim for a saturated fat intake of not more than ten per cent.

Sometimes recommendations are made about changing the ratio between polyunsaturates and saturates in the diet.[6] It has been suggested that the polyunsaturates and saturates should provide the same proportion of fat, say eight to ten per cent of each with the remainder made up of monounsaturates. Very high concentrations of polyunsaturates are not to be recommended, however, since this lowers levels of the 'good' HDL cholesterol.

It's not easy to calculate precise figures for intake of fat because of all the hidden fats in our food. Your dietitian will be able to help you to work out percentages if you are following a supervised diet and keeping a 'food diary'. However, if you are trying to follow a reduced fat diet on your own, the best advice is to start by cutting down on all fats, and then aim to reduce your intake of saturated fat by substituting monounsaturates and some polyunsaturates. This will help to keep your weight down and your blood-fat levels healthy.

Fibre

It is well known that dietary fibre is necessary for a healthy digestive system and to prevent a variety of ailments such as constipation, bowel cancer, haemorrhoids, and diverticular disease. What is less well known is that fibre is also a key element in the fight against raised cholesterol levels, and hence against heart disease.

Dietary fibre consists of the largely indigestible carbohydrates obtained from foods of plant origin. It is found in the fibrous parts of fruit, vegetables, cereals, beans, and pulses. For practical purposes, it is useful to divide dietary fibre into two types: soluble and insoluble.[7]

Soluble fibre

The actual substances are gums, gels, and pectins, and they are extremely good for lowering cholesterol levels. They are found in:

- most fruits and vegetables;
- cereals such as oats, barley, and rye;
- pulses like beans, peas, lentils and chick peas.

The soluble fibre is dissolved in the watery fluids within the digestive system, but it does not break down sufficiently to be absorbed into the bloodstream. It tends to form a kind of sticky gel that slows down the passage of food through the body (but without producing constipation), a feature that is particularly valuable for people with diabetes, since it helps to slow the rate at which sugar is released into the blood after digestion. Soluble fibre also helps to retain some of the bile acids and prevent them being reabsorbed, and it is eventually passed out of the body, together with the bile acids, in the stools. The effect of this process is that more of the liver-produced cholesterol is used up in order to replace the 'lost' bile (you may remember that one of the functions of cholesterol is to make bile). Hence the level of cholesterol in the blood will tend to fall.

Oats, and particularly oatbran (the fibrous outer layer of the oat), are a particularly good source of soluble fibre. The oats themselves, either as rolled oats or oatmeal (finely chopped oats), will contain on average 30 per cent of oatbran, but it is also possible to buy oatbran on its own (Chapter 13 includes a recipe for an appetizing fruity oatbran bun). Because of their high soluble fibre content, oat products have been used in a large number of research studies examining the relationship between diet and cholesterol. The main outcome of this research is that oat products in general, and oatbran products in particular, are beneficial in lowering cholesterol levels. As far as oatbran is concerned, several studies have shown that a regular intake of somewhere in the region of 50g daily (less in some studies, more in others) can be effective in lowering total cholesterol levels. It should be noted, though, that wheatbran does not have a cholesterol-lowering effect, since this is an insoluble fibre.

Insoluble fibre

Insoluble fibre is what is often described as roughage and, although it doesn't dissolve, it will absorb water and swell up to give bulk to the stools and help to keep them soft. Hence, it is especially important for people who have problems with constipation, and, as we have already seen, it has a protective effect against diseases of the bowel. This is where wheatbran, wholegrain cereals, and wholemeal bread come into their own, together with fibrous fruit and vegetables. With high-fibre diets, however, it is important to make sure that the fluid intake is also kept up, and it is wise to avoid an excessive intake of 'neat' fibre, since too much insoluble fibre can prevent the absorption of other nutrients in your food. It is better to go for a range of fibre, including a variety of the soluble dietary fibre described earlier.

Anti-oxidants

Another plus for foods high in dietary fibre, such as fruit and vegetables, is that many of them are also rich in certain nutrients that may play an important role in keeping cholesterol in check. These nutrients are:

1 beta-carotene (a form of vitamin A);
2 vitamin C;
3 vitamin E;
4 selenium.

They are sometimes referred to collectively as *anti-oxidants*. We're all familiar with the effects of oxidization on food. For example, when fat goes rancid this is due to oxidization, and anti-oxidants help to prevent this process occurring. The same thing can happen to our body fats, and when cholesterol is oxidized it becomes much easier for it to cling to the walls of the arteries and clog them. (Incidently, cholesterol tends to oxidize more rapidly with a high intake of polyunsaturates, as opposed to monoun-saturates, so this is another reason for encouraging the use of monounsaturated oils in our diet.) The process of oxidization is also encouraged by some chemical 'agents' called *free radicals* that are implicated in a number of diseases including cancer. Anti-oxidants help to 'mop up' the free radicals in our bodies; and whether the effects are related to the anti-oxidant elements or to other hitherto unresearched properties of the foods involved, what is abundantly clear from research studies around the world is that people who have a high consumption of anti-oxidant foods such as fruit and vegetables tend to have a lower risk of cancer and cardio-vascular disease.

Fortunately, the foods containing the anti-oxidant vitamins are tasty and readily available.

1 Beta-carotene

As far as beta-carotene is concerned, this refers to the orange pigment found in green, yellow and orange vegetables. Carrots and dark green vegetables (such as spinach) contain the highest amounts, but it is present in a wide variety of fruits and vegetables, especially apricots, mangoes, sweet melons, red peppers, broccoli, watercress and lettuce. It is not destroyed by cooking.

2 Vitamin C

Vitamin C (ascorbic acid) is also widely available in fresh fruit and vegetables, but is more or less absent from grains, meat and fats (apart from whale blubber!) Particularly good sources of vitamin C are citrus fruits, blackcurrants, strawberries, guavas, broccoli, greens, parsley, peppers and new potatoes. Vitamin C is partly destroyed by cooking, though, and smokers have lower levels of Vitamin C in their blood than non-smokers.

3 Vitamin E

Good sources of vitamin E are vegetable oils (especially sunflower seed oil), wholemeal cereals, leafy vegetables and nuts. (The cholesterol-lowering properties of nuts will also be discussed more fully later on.) Like beta-carotene, vitamin E is not destroyed by cooking.

4 Selenium

This is a trace element that can be found in a number of food sources, including cereals, fish and nuts (especially brazils and walnuts).

(Tomato sauce is also rich in anti-oxidants, as is red wine, a point discussed in the next chapter.)

Table 2 Fat content of selected nuts

Type of nut	Predominant type of fat	Proportion saturated fat
Coconut	Saturated	Over 90 per cent
Hazelnuts	Monounsaturated	
Almonds	" "	Less than 10 per cent
Pecan nuts	" "	
Cashew nuts	Monounsaturated	
Brazil nuts	" "	Between 20–25 per cent
Walnuts	Polyunsaturated	
Pine nuts	" "	Less than 10 per cent
Sunflower seeds	" "	

Nuts

As we have seen, nuts provide a food source for vitamin E and selenium, but they are also effective cholesterol-lowering foods in their own right. All nuts (with the exception of chestnuts) are high in fat, so intake needs to be controlled from the weight-control angle; but the sort of fat tends to be predominantly unsaturated. The main exception to this rule is coconut, which is highly saturated, and should be avoided by people with cholesterol problems. The fat in most other nuts, however, is largely monoun-saturated or polyunsaturated, as can be seen in Table 2. So the predominance of monounsaturated or polyunsaturated fat in nuts tends to make them a very useful component in a cholesterol-lowering diet, and there is research evidence that supports their effectiveness.

Case study JOAN

Joan is 54, married, and has three grown-up children. She works part-time as a check-out operator at the local supermarket, and used to enjoy the work very much. She had been feeling rather tense for some time, however, and found that she couldn't concentrate very well at work. Her periods had been irregular for a few years, and had now more or less stopped; she had suffered from unpleasant hot flushes and 'night sweats' for some time, and she found sex painful. Her husband, Tony, suggested she went to the doctor. He'd read in a magazine at the dentist's about the menopause, and how HRT can sometimes help middle-aged women. He thought that Joan seemed to be having exactly the same sort of symptoms as the women described in the article, and suggested she ask the doctor if HRT was worth a try.

The GP was sympathetic to the idea. He was sure that Joan's symptoms were menopausal, but he gave her a thorough examination and also suggested that she should have a routine blood test for cholesterol. He explained that although women tend to have lower cholesterol than men during their younger years, this situation changes after the menopause. The GP thought that HRT would definitely be worth a try, both to relieve her symptoms and to protect her from heart disease. He commented rather bluntly that more women die of heart disease than any other disease, despite the fact that a lot of people seem to think it's only a problem for men. As he wrote out the prescription, he also mentioned a further advantage of HRT, in that it helps to protect women from osteoporosis, the thinning or weakening of the bones that occurs as a result of a depletion of calcium in their bodies. He explained that osteoporosis tends to be most pronounced in small-boned, relatively inactive, post-menopausal women who smoke. Although Joan doesn't smoke and gets quite a bit of exercise walking to and from work, she qualifies as a candidate for osteoporosis on the other two counts, so she was pleased to think that the HRT might also help to keep her bones stronger.

When she went back to discuss the results of the blood test, the doctor told her that her total cholesterol level was 7.6 mmol/l – 'a high-risk score'. He asked her about her diet, and then suggested that she should cut down on fatty foods, and keep the saturated fat content under ten per cent if possible.

Joan mentioned that it might be difficult for her to change her diet a great deal. She usually fitted in with her husband's choice of food to make cooking easier – and he was a 'fried breakfast, chips with everything man' who wasn't keen on fruit and vegetables. The GP suggested she should grill food instead of frying it, and use monounsaturated or polyunsaturated cooking oils. Despite her misgivings, Joan agreed to have a go, and she'd also see if she could persuade her husband to come down for a check-up, as the doctor suggested.

She had a bit of a problem convincing Tony that they should try a low-fat diet, but she dragged him out on a 'supermarket crawl' to hunt out a few low-fat versions of his favourite foods. His eyes lit up when he found some chips with less than five per cent fat. Joan also pointed out that the saturated fat content was less than one per cent! Instead of buying ordinary cheddar cheese, they bought some low-fat sunflower cheese; instead of lard, they bought a bottle of blended vegetable oil, high in monounsaturates and polyunsaturates and low in saturates; they tried to choose low-fat varieties of most of the other fat-containing food items, apart from milk. They'd tried skimmed milk once before and didn't like the 'watery taste'. Although Tony wasn't keen, Joan also bought rather more fruit and vegetables than usual. To keep down the price of the weekly shopping basket, they also decided to have a go at growing some potatoes, lettuces, and runner beans. They'd never done it before, but their neighbours reckoned they saved pounds on their shopping bills during the summer by growing some of their own vegetables.

The HRT had a dramatic effect on Joan's menopausal

symptoms. She felt much less tense, her hot flushes and night sweats lessened, and she could even enjoy sex now because the vaginal dryness had miraculously disappeared. Despite a few grumbles about 'Mediterranean' food, Tony also seemed to quite enjoy his new diet – though he didn't say that to the lads down at the pub! Joan hadn't so far managed to get him to the surgery for a cholesterol check, but he had lost nearly half a stone in weight and he'd promised to go 'sometime next summer'. When Joan had her first six-monthly check-up, her cholesterol had gone down to 6.2 mmol/l, which put her in the 'moderate' rather than 'high-risk' category for developing coronary heart disease. The practice nurse was very pleased with this drop in level, and she made a few suggestions about how she might reduce the level even more ('we're aiming for something around 5.2 if you can make it'). She suggested that Joan and Tony should add a bit more fibre to their diet – wholemeal bread, muesli or porridge for breakfast, that sort of thing. And since they weren't keen on skimmed milk, she suggested they should change to semi-skimmed milk to begin with. The nurse also suggested that it would be a good idea if she did some slightly more strenuous exercise, like swimming, or walking more briskly to work – 'something that gets you a little out of breath'. She explained about the two types of cholesterol and how this sort of exercise will help to increase the 'good' HDL cholesterol, and generally improve fitness.

On her next visit, in the late summer, Joan's cholesterol was down to 5.5. She was really chuffed. She felt better than she'd felt for years, and her figure was nearly as trim as it had been in her thirties (she could even get into her daughter's size 12 jeans!). Flushed with her own success, Joan decided before she left the surgery to make a provisional appointment for Tony to have his promised 'summer' cholesterol test!

We have seen in this chapter how our choices of foods with different types of fat and fibre content will affect levels of cholesterol. In the next chapter we continue our examination of nutritional issues by looking at drinks, food supplements, and some special diets.

8

Lowering cholesterol by diet (2): drinks, supplements, and special diets

In this chapter we shall look at the effects of different types of drinks on blood-fat levels, paying particular attention to the evidence about alcohol and coffee; then we shall examine the value of certain dietary supplements, including vitamins and garlic; finally, we shall look at the main components of three special diets – the Step 1 and 2 diets, vegetarian diets, and finally the Mediterranean diet.

Drinks

Just as different types of food can have different effects on our blood fat levels, so can different kinds of drink.

Milk

We have already seen that we can reduce the saturated fat content of milk by changing to skimmed or semi-skimmed varieties. As can be seen in Table 1, whole milk usually has about four per cent fat content, nearly two-thirds of which is saturated. Semi-skimmed milk, on the other hand, has less than half the saturated fat content of whole milk, and skimmed milk has only about 0.1 per cent of fat in total!

You have to be a bit careful about powdered milks (the sort you can use to sprinkle on coffee or tea), since some of these are quite high in saturated fat. Similarly, drinks that can be made up with milk also sometimes have a high saturated content. The only certain way of knowing the saturated fat content of any particular item, of course, is to check the food label; and don't give up hope of finding a suitable replacement for a favourite drink that turns out to be full of saturated fat. For example, you can buy packets of instant hot chocolate containing under three per cent fat, and only about half of this saturated.

Table 1 Typical fat content of milk and other selected dairy products

	Total fat per 100g	Percentage saturated fat
Evaporated milk	9.4	5.9
Whole milk	3.9	2.4
Semi-skimmed	1.6	1.0
Skimmed	0.1	<0.1
Double cream	48.0	30.0
Whipping cream	39.3	24.6
Single cream	19.1	11.9
Greek style yoghurt	10.2	6.2
Whole milk yoghurt	3.0	1.7
Low fat yoghurt	1.0	0.6
Cream cheese	47.4	29.7
Stilton	35.5	22.2
Hard cheese – average (e.g. Cheddar, Derby Double Gloucester, Leicester)	34.0	21.3
Brie	26.9	16.8
Edam	25.4	15.9
Half fat cheddar	16.5	10.5
Low fat fromage frais	0.2	0.1
Half fat cottage cheese	0.9	0.6
Quark	0.2	0.1

Soft drinks

Most soft drinks are virtually fat-free, but you will have to watch the sugar content if your body isn't good at coping with too much sugar, e.g. if you are diabetic. Again, the only way of checking is to look on the nutritional labels.

Alcohol and coffee

There has been a good deal of discussion about the effects of alcohol and coffee on cholesterol levels, and much of the discussion has been ill-informed.

Alcohol

As far as alcohol is concerned, it has some distinctly beneficial effects on blood-fat levels. In particular, it helps to raise levels of the 'good' HDL cholesterol, which in turn helps to increase protection against coronary heart disease. Alcohol also provides further ammunition in the fight against heart disease in that it lowers fibrinogen levels and hence reduces the tendency of blood to clot. This is probably why teetotallers tend to have a higher risk of developing heart disease than moderate drinkers. An additional bonus is also offered for people who drink red wine (the mealtime drink favoured in the Mediterranean diet discussed later). This is due to the fact that it has a high concentration of some potent anti-oxidants called *polyphenols*, especially phenolic flavonoids. (These flavonoids, which help to suppress the oxidization of lipids, are also found to a lesser extent in white wine, in other drinks such as grape juice and tea, and in vegetables and fruit, especially onions and apples.) It has been suggested in fact that the anti-clotting/anti-oxidant properties of red wine, together with the other cholesterol-lowering and anti-oxidant elements of the Mediterranean diet, go some way to explaining the 'French paradox' – the fact that the French have a low incidence of coronary heart disease, despite a diet that includes considerable amounts of saturated fat, e.g. soft cheeses. (Though since some soft French cheeses such as camembert are also rich in folic acid which lowers levels of homocysteine in the blood and hence helps to reduce risk levels for heart disease (see page 130), they may be another contributory factor in explaining the French paradox!)

The downside with alcohol is the fact that an increased intake of it tends to stimulate the body's production of triglyceride. Over-indulgence in alcohol is also associated with sudden death and strokes. So a sensible intake of alcohol will help to increase your HDL levels, and red wine will act as an anti-oxidant, thus offering an element of protection against heart disease. Drinking too much alcohol, on the other hand, will inflict heavy damage on your liver, and at the same time increase your risk of having a stroke or sudden cardiac arrest.

Fortunately, there are some straightforward guidelines for sensible drinking, and the detrimental effects of too much alcohol can be avoided if these are adhered to (see Chapter 9).

Coffee

Both coffee and tea contain caffeine (as does coca-cola, which has about half the amount contained in tea, and also cocoa and drinking chocolate, which have about a tenth of that in tea). Ground coffee has the highest amount, with instant coffee next, and tea coming third. Caffeine is a relatively non-toxic substance, but it stimulates the heart and central nervous system. Too much caffeine can result in side effects such as palpitations and sleeplessness, but there is no convincing evidence to suggest that it causes heart disease. Of the two main caffeine containing drinks, tea has received a relatively 'good press' – quite justifiably, since there is no evidence that it has any negative effects on the cardio-vascular system, and there is even some evidence that suggests it might have a lipid-lowering effect! Coffee, on the other hand, has been hounded as a possible cause of raised cholesterol and increased risk of coronary heart disease. The concern about coffee is understandable, since some forms of coffee have been found to raise cholesterol levels; but it is the method of brewing the coffee rather than the amount of caffeine involved that seems to be the crucial factor.

To summarize the position as far as coffee and cholesterol is concerned:

- Caffeine does not appear to be a significant factor in raising cholesterol, although it can cause palpitations and sleeplessness, particularly if drunk in excess (six or more cups a day); and remember that instant coffee has much less caffeine than ground coffee.
- From a cholesterol point of view, there is no benefit to be gained from drinking decaffeinated as opposed to caffeinated coffee (and some studies have shown that a change to decaffeinated coffee has actually led to an increase in cholesterol levels!).
- Instant coffee and filter coffee do not generally have any strong effect on cholesterol levels; and in the Scottish Heart Health Study it was found that regular coffee drinkers (mainly consuming instant coffee) tended to have less heart disease than people who drank little or no coffee.
- Boiled coffee (in which the coffee grounds are left to soak in boiling water as in the cafetière method, or actually boiled repeatedly as in the Scandinavian method) does raise cholesterol levels, but the cholesterol-raising substance is largely removed by filter methods such as the use of filter papers.

Dietary supplements

In general, we don't need supplements; our diets may not be perfectly balanced, but they usually provide the essential nutrients that our bodies require in order to function adequately. However, when we are helping our bodies to cope with specific problems, such as raised cholesterol, there may be a need to consider increasing or decreasing the intake of certain foods (as we have already discussed) or supplementing our diets in certain ways.

As far as vitamin supplements are concerned, there is usually little point in adding these to our diet unless there is some reason to suspect a deficiency. If you follow a vegan diet (i.e. one containing no food of animal origin at all) then you will need to check that you are having an adequate intake of vitamin B12. However, for vegetarians who eat milk and eggs, there is unlikely to be any deficiency in this particular vitamin. Even with a vegan diet it does not present a problem, providing you eat some foods with enhanced vitamin B12 content – such as yeast extracts or breakfast cereals supplemented with this vitamin. If oily fish isn't eaten, then some form of supplement may also be necessary to obtain an adequate supply of vitamin D, but again some margarines and breakfast cereals are fortified with it.

The main vitamin supplement that has been shown in research studies to be effective in the prevention of cardio-vascular problems is vitamin E. In the USA, two very large samples of subjects, free of diagnosed heart disease at the beginning of the research, were assessed for habitual levels of vitamin intake and then followed through for several years. A group of 40,000 middle-aged male health professionals was followed up for four years, and a sample of 87,000 female nurses for eight years. In analysing the data it was found in both studies that those taking higher doses of vitamin E supplements for long periods (at least two years) showed a reduced risk of coronary heart disease after adjustment for coronary risk factors, age, and intake of other anti-oxidant nutrients. In Britain, the Cambridge Heart Antioxidant Study (CHAOS) has also shown that treatment by vitamin E supplement can help reduce the rate of non-fatal heart attacks in patients with coronary atherosclerosis. The value of maintaining a good intake of vitamin E *from food* has also been demonstrated in another study involving over 30,000 post-menopausal women in the USA. This showed a clear reduction in risk of death from coronary heart disease as level of intake of vitamin E increased, and this was particularly striking in women who did not take vitamin supplements but relied on their intake of vitamin E from food. This is not to say, of course, that everyone ought to be taking extra amounts of vitamin E, but it does seem that there is considerable benefit to be gained from ensuring a good intake of vitamin E from food, and that supplements, *where considered medically necessary*, may provide an element of protection against heart disease.

The same cannot be said about another supplement that has been marketed in recent years as a cholesterol-lowering agent. This is *lecithin*, a collective name for several fatty substances found in the cells of all plants and animals, which act like 'wetting agents' or emulsifiers helping to suspend globules of fat in liquids. It had been hoped that lecithin might help to suspend cholesterol in the blood and so render it less likely to be deposited on the walls of the arteries, but this has not turned out to be the case. Unfortunately, when lecithin is eaten it tends to be broken down into other substances, and thus its effectiveness as a 'wetting agent' is nullified. So it's thumbs down for lecithin! Similarly, despite clear evidence that the intake of food high in anti-oxidants has protective effects against various diseases, the use of large unsupervised doses of anti-oxidant supplements is not a practice to be recommended. Our level of scientific knowledge about the interactive effects of large doses of supplements is still in its infancy, and there is some evidence to suggest that in some circumstances high doses of certain vitamins may even be harmful.

Garlic on the other hand, is a different story, and there is a substantial body of evidence to suggest that this substance, both in its natural form and as a supplement, can be a valuable agent in the fight against diseases of the heart and blood vessels. It appears that garlic possesses anti-oxidant properties, and that, like onions, it can act as an anti-coagulant (i.e. it stops blood clotting). Studies have also shown that it can help to fight bacteria, control blood pressure, reduce levels of fibrinogen, triglyceride and LDL cholesterol, whilst raising the 'good' HDL. Until recently, the potential of garlic as a health-promoting agent has been largely unexplored by the traditional medical profession. There have been one or two small-scale clinical research studies which have suggested that garlic treatment might have a less pronounced effect on cholesterol levels than previously indicated but there is a strong and consistent trend in the overall research findings which shows that garlic does seem to offer some beneficial effects on the cardio-vascular system in general and on lipid levels in particular. Indeed the medical profession in Germany is sufficiently convinced of the case for garlic that doctors in that country have for some time been able to prescribe garlic tablets containing dried garlic as a medicine for lowering cholesterol.

It is not entirely clear which active ingredients in garlic account for its apparent value as a cholesterol-lowering agent, but the most likely agent is *allicin*, the substance that produces the familiar garlic odour. If you smell a fresh garlic clove before crushing it, you will find that it is more or less odourless, and it is only when the garlic is cut that the taste and odour appear. Chinese garlic has a particularly high allicin yield.[1] Garlic oil products, on the other hand, are made by a distillation process that removes most of the allicin. If allicin does turn out to be the main ingredient in garlic responsible for its cholesterol-lowering and other beneficial effects, it would seem sensible for people taking garlic as a supplement to stick to those preparations having the highest allicin yield (i.e. garlic tablets made from garlic powder). The only problem with these tablets, however, is that they can make your breath smell. So, in addition to anti-oxidant and anti-coagulant properties, they can also be somewhat anti-social! The point is, though, that the odour problem can sometimes represent a drawback to use, since even 'odour-controlled' tablets, when taken in large doses, tend to produce a recognizable odour on the breath in about 20 per cent of cases. If you're one of the 20 per cent, you may simply have to balance the advantages of a better blood-fats level with the disadvantages of the odour!

Sometimes the use of garlic as a form of treatment is rejected because it is thought that it is necessary to take massive amounts either in the raw form or as tablets in order to produce any substantial effects. However, there is convincing evidence that relatively small quantities (i.e. one to three cloves a day) are beneficial and good results can be obtained using quite manageable quantities of garlic tablets (e.g. 600–800 mg of dried garlic in total per day).[2] A dosage of 800 mg, for example, has been shown to lower total cholesterol by over 10 per cent, the greatest effect being observed when the initial level of cholesterol was in the range 6.5 to 7.8 mmol/l. This dosage also reduced triglycerides by 17 per cent and blood pressure by 12 per cent.

So the message seems to be that garlic is good for you, and the use of good quality fresh garlic in cooking is the best way to ensure a pleasurable and beneficial intake; however, supplements are also worth a try if you're not making as much headway as you would like through diet alone.

Special diets

Vegetarian diets

Vegetarian diets are generally very good for people with cholesterol problems (and also for people without such problems!). The high content of cholesterol-lowering foods often found in such diets (e.g. vegetables, pulses, nuts, fruit and oat-based muesli) is clearly beneficial for keeping cholesterol in check. A vegetable-rich diet also ensures that you are getting plenty of the essential vitamins (especially the anti-oxidant vitamins we have already discussed), and to ensure that these are not lost in cooking it's best to microwave, stir-fry, or steam. For the 'vegetarian' who still eats fish, there are also added benefits – particularly if oily fish is eaten regularly, since (as we have already seen) this has the potential for keeping triglycerides and blood pressure in check.

The effectiveness of non-meat-eating diets in helping to maintain good health and increase longevity has been demonstrated in numerous research studies in this country and abroad. One German study, for example, in which subjects were followed up over an 11-year period, found that mortality from all causes was reduced by one-half in the vegetarian group compared with that in the population at large. The lowest mortality was found for cardio-vascular disease, but deaths from respiratory and digestive disorders were also reduced by a half, and cancer deaths by between a quarter to a half. In Britain, the Oxford Vegetarian Study showed a 40 per cent reduction in cancer deaths in non-meat-eaters as compared with meat-eaters after other factors, such as smoking, had been taken into account. Deaths from coronary heart disease showed a comparable reduction among non-meat-eaters, with death rates about a quarter that of the general population; though this finding may be related in part to the non-dietary factors that tend to be associated with vegetarians, such as a low body mass index (i.e. a trim figure!) and a healthy, non-smoking lifestyle. But it's clear that, in general, a well-balanced, non-meat-eating diet helps to reduce mortality rates in its own right.

The Step 1 and 2 diets

In essence, both these diets (originating from the USA) are lipid-lowering, but the saturated fat content in the Step 2 diet is seven per cent – compared with ten per cent in the Step 1 diet. Also, the dietary cholesterol allowed is 300 mg in the Step 1 diet, but 200 mg per day in Step 2.

Except for a few people with severe blood fat conditions the role of dietary cholesterol is not very significant. For example, most people can eat two or three egg yolks a week, without adversely affecting their levels of blood cholesterol.[3]

Since it is usually recommended that anyone with cholesterol problems should follow the elements of the Step 1 diet to begin with, its main features are set out in Table 2. When using this sort of diet sheet, it's important not to use it simply as the basis for a 'denial diet' – in which you concentrate only on cutting out inadvisable foods. Instead, use it in a positive manner by selecting as wide a range of 'good food choices' as you can find, so that you enjoy a nutritious and varied diet. It is also worth remembering that by spreading your intake of cholesterol-lowering foods throughout the day (for example, by eating three smaller meals rather than one large one), you will be helping your body to deal more effectively with both weight and blood-fat problems. The Family Heart Association produces a useful *Guide to Healthy Eating* that offers detailed advice on food choices. You can also contact the FHA for advice on specific food products. The FHA address is given on page 121.

The Mediterranean diet

The diet of people in such parts of Europe as the south of France, southern Italy and Greece constitutes what has become known as the Mediterranean diet, and this is the type of diet that comes closest to meeting the World Health Organization guidelines for healthy eating. It is also in these Mediterranean areas that coronary heart disease rates tend to be the lowest in Europe; it seems likely that this is no coincidence, since their diet contains most of the cholesterol-lowering elements that we have discussed earlier in this chapter.

Table 2 Basic lipid-lowering diet (slightly modified version of Step 1 diet – includes essential elements plus some added examples)

Food group	Choose	Best to avoid
Breads and cereals	Wholemeal breads and cereals (e.g. oats, rye, bran, crispbreads) Home-made baked foods using unsaturated oils sparingly Rice and pasta	Commercially baked items with high saturated fat content found in many bought pies, cakes and biscuits
Fats and oils	Very low fat content generally; unsaturated vegetable oils; margarines high in unsaturates, low in trans-fatty acids (spread thinly); low-fat dressings	Butter, coconut and palm oil, dripping, suet, lard; high-fat mayonnaise (but there are some very low-fat mayonnaise-style dressings available); cream sauces
Dairy produce	Skimmed milk, low-fat yoghurt; low-fat cottage cheese; very low-fat ice cream	Whole milk, cream and hard cheeses high in saturates; ice cream high in saturates
Eggs	Egg whites; two to three whole eggs per week in total (i.e including those in cakes, puddings, etc.)	Excess of egg yolks

Fruit and vegetables	All fresh, frozen, or tinned (in natural juices), fruit and vegetables, including salads; at least five helpings a day recommended (in addition to potatoes, which, for fibre, are best eaten as jacket potatoes)	Greasy chips cooked in saturated fat
Nuts and seeds	Most nuts – but note that nuts tend to be high in fat, so have high calorie count	Coconut
Fish and meat	Fish generally (including shellfish occasionally, despite cholesterol content)[4]; oily fish such as tuna and mackerel; lean cuts of meat	Fish roe (high in cholesterol) All fatty cuts of meat and meat pies
Drinks	Skimmed milk, tea, instant or filter coffee, fruit juice (unsweetened); mineral water; alcohol in moderation; soups low in saturates	Powdered milk for coffee/tea; cream soups high in saturates

The essential elements of the Mediterranean diet are:

- plenty of complex carbohydrates such as bread, potatoes, pasta, rice;
- plenty of fresh fruit and vegetables, eaten raw or lightly cooked;
- plenty of fresh salads;
- using a highly monounsaturated oil (such as olive oil) rather than saturated fats;
- grilling, steaming, or baking, rather than deep frying;
- eating white and oily fish, and small quantities of lean cuts of meat;
- using garlic liberally in all sorts of cooking;
- using plenty of other herbs and spices (but remember to cut levels of salt to a minimum);
- enjoying wine (and especially red wine) in moderation with meals.

Mealtimes also tend to be taken at a leisurely rate in Mediterranean countries (with a good break at lunchtime and in the evening). This aids digestion and allows the alcohol to be absorbed more slowly than on an empty stomach. The Mediterranean approach also encourages us to savour and enjoy the food we are eating – and when it is realized that the diet is also helping to provide protection against heart disease, it becomes literally a life-enhancing experience!

9

Lifestyle changes (1): exercise, sensible drinking, and weight-watching

Attention to diet is likely to be the cornerstone of treatment in most cases of raised blood fats, but there are a number of other lifestyle changes that can help and among the most important are healthy exercise, weight-watching, sensible drinking, coping with stress, and stopping smoking. The first three will be covered in this chapter, and ways of coping with stress and stopping smoking will be dealt with in Chapter 10. Combined with healthy eating habits, lifestyle changes can be extremely effective in combating cholesterol problems, and there is evidence to show that such combined measures may also be important in bringing about regression (reduction) of coronary atherosclerosis.

Healthy exercise

It might seem odd to talk about 'healthy' exercise – isn't all exercise healthy? The answer is usually 'yes', but sometimes it is 'no'. It depends upon the physical condition of the exerciser and the nature of the exercise. In general, regular exercise is beneficial as part of a cholesterol-lowering and stress-reducing lifestyle. It will help to keep your weight (and triglycerides) down and the 'good' HDLs up, and can reduce the risk of heart attacks to as much as half that of non-exercisers. However, certain types of exercise are not recommended for some people because their fitness levels are not sufficiently good to withstand the physical stress. To take an obvious example, it's not a good idea for somebody who is middle-aged, has high-risk factors for heart disease, has taken no regular exercise previously, and works in a sedentary occupation, suddenly to start playing energetic games of squash! There's a chance that it will help to raise HDL levels, but there's also a chance that it will increase the risk of a heart attack! So, the first message is to engage in exercise at a level that is appropriate for your present state of physical fitness, and to increase your level of activity at a gentle pace. The right level of exercise should make you get a little out of breath, so that you can see that your heart and lungs are having a work-out, but it should also leave you feeling invigorated and with an enhanced sense of 'well-being'. Your GP, practice nurse, or physiotherapist will be able to advise you on the types of exercise suitable for you, but there are also some general guidelines that can help.

There are two main types of exercise: *isometric* and *aerobic*. Isometric exercise involves 'straining' tasks such as weight-lifting. It can be very useful in toning up the muscles, but it can also have the effect of unhealthily increasing systolic blood pressure. Therefore, this type of exercise is not to be recommended for the older age groups, and anyone suffering from high blood pressure.

Aerobic exercise, on the other hand, aims to improve fitness through increased oxygen consumption, and it is useful for all age groups. The type of exercises involved are those that increase your breathing rate and get you slightly puffed, like brisk walking, swimming, jogging, dancing, cycling, and sporting activities such as tennis and badminton. These are generally safe provided that you exercise at your own pace, and select activities in line with your current state of fitness. But remember, always be guided by what your own body is telling you; and if you feel pain or discomfort, then stop exercising straightaway.

The aim with exercise is to start at a gentle pace and to work up gradually to a level that gets you a little puffed; and to be of benefit to your heart, you need to try to exercise at this sort of level (the 'breathing hard' level) for about 30 minutes, five days a week. Remember also that you don't need to be in the sports hall or swimming pool to exercise in this way and you don't need to do it all in one go! Brisk walking is one of the best forms of aerobic exercise, and you can look out for opportunities of doing a bit more walking or using other forms of energetic exercise while carrying out your everyday chores. Some examples might be:

- leaving your car at home for the short journey to the local shops and back;
- getting off the bus or tube a stop early;
- taking your dog for a longer walk each day;
- using the stairs instead of the lift or escalator;
- cycling instead of driving where possible.

Weight-watching

If you pay attention to your diet, exercise regularly, and keep your consumption of alcohol to reasonable limits, then you are unlikely to run into serious weight problems – the sort associated with high blood pressure, low HDLs, raised triglycerides, and increased risk of coronary heart disease. If you are unsure of the appropriate weight for your height, Figure 2 (opposite) offers a general guide.

If you are overweight, you should aim for a slow, steady weight loss rather than going on a crash diet. Something like 1 kg (about 2lb) a week represents a reasonable maximum target for most people, which means consuming something like 500–750 calories less each day than your present intake. It's not always easy to calculate your calorie intake, but keeping a 'food diary' for a period (together with a weekly weight chart to show your progress) would help, and, if you're getting nutritional advice, the dietitian will help to work out the figures for you.

Try to change your eating habits to take in the sort of approach described in the previous two chapters. This will involve a healthy and enjoyable eating style rather than a negative 'cut out all fattening foods' regime – though you may well need to trim a few of your more spectacular over-indulgences initially! Doing exercise is certainly valuable for people who are slightly overweight. However, if you are very overweight, it is important to get medical advice on the type of exercise that would be most beneficial.

Sensible drinking

We have seen that some alcohol can be beneficial for people with cholesterol problems, but there are clear dangers associated with drinking too much (see Chapters 3 and 8). The use of alcohol as an accompaniment at mealtimes – for example, a glass of red wine as part of the Mediterranean diet – can be seen as a pleasure that is also doing you good! It is very important, though, to follow the recommended guidelines for sensible drinking, and to understand these we need to think in terms of units of alcohol consumed, where one unit contains 10 ml of pure alcohol. In 'pub' measures, one unit of alcohol is roughly equivalent to:

- half a pint of ordinary strength beer, lager, or cider;
- a small glass of wine (11 per cent alcohol);

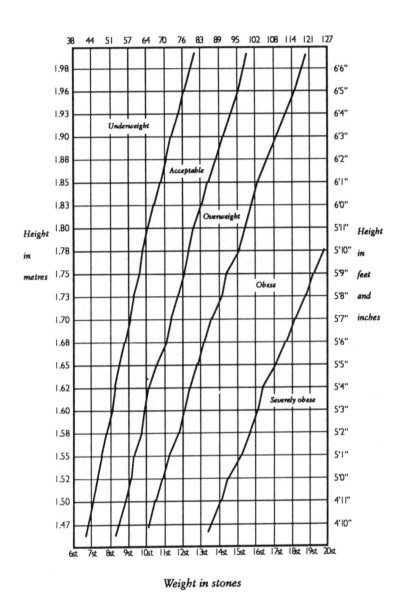

Figure 2 Body mass index (BMI) chart[1]

- a single measure of spirits (40 per cent alcohol);
- a small glass of sherry, port, or vermouth.

Home measures of spirits, which tend to be larger than pub measures, should be counted as two units; and remember that it takes our bodies approximately 1 to 1½ hours (generally longer for women than men) to break down each unit of alcohol consumed.

The recommended *maximum* limits for sensible drinking are:

- three to four units of alcohol per day for men;
- two to three units of alcohol per day for women;
  and preferably
- two alcohol-free days per week for both men and women.

These recommended maximum limits are somewhat controversial, however, and many medical experts consider that the best advice for most people (and certainly for people with cholesterol problems) would be to keep within the *lower* limits.

Any consumption of alcohol is best accompanied by food, and the occasions spread out rather than indulging in one long 'drinking binge'. Women need to stick to lower limits more than men because they tend to be lighter, have smaller livers, and break down alcohol more slowly, and heavy alcohol consumption during pregnancy (eight units per day or more) will damage the foetus.

It should also be remembered that it is easy to underestimate the number of units being drunk because of the differences in the percentage of alcohol contained in various drinks and the range of glass sizes used. So, in other words, one can or glass doesn't necessarily represent just one unit – you need to take note of the ABV (alcohol by volume) values on the label, and the glass, bottle, or can size to establish the number of units you are drinking.[2]

10

Lifestyle changes (2): dealing with stress and stopping smoking

We have seen that stress can raise cholesterol levels, and that people who exhibit some aspects of Type A behaviour (particularly the tendency to react to stress with 'bottled-up' anger and hostility) are likely to be particularly prone to coronary heart disease (see Chapter 3). In looking at lifestyle changes, therefore, it is helpful to look at ways of coping more successfully with stressful situations. Some of these will be examined in the first part of this chapter, and then we will go on to consider ways of stopping smoking – a challenge that remains for many people the key to keeping at bay coronary heart disease, as well as several other life-threatening diseases.

Dealing with stress

You need a certain amount of stress to keep you alert and on your toes! However, when the level of stress becomes too great, you will begin to suffer physical and psychological symptoms. Adrenalin surges round your body, your blood pressure rises, and your heart begins to pump more forcefully as it gets ready to fight or escape – the so-called 'fight or flight' reaction. You may experience other symptoms too: your mouth becomes dry and throat restricted, your hands and knees may begin to shake, or your voice tremble, your stomach is 'tied in knots' or 'turns over', you may feel as if a tight band has been tied around your forehead, and you start to sweat.

Such reactions are to be expected in 'threatening' situations, and they usually subside when the initial threat passes. However, when such reactions refuse to subside after the 'danger' has receded, or when your life has too many 'threatening' features in it and the reactions have become a permanent part of your everyday life, then stress has got out of hand. As we have seen, too much stress will tend to raise blood pressure, increase the blood's tendency to clot, raise total cholesterol scores, and lower the 'good' HDL levels, thus ensuring an overall increase in the risk of developing coronary heart disease. So in this sort of situation it's a good idea to consider ways of changing your lifestyle to reduce the stress, and to learn techniques for dealing with your feelings of tension.

Changing your lifestyle

The first thing to do if you appear to have a permanently over-stressful existence is to step back and take a look at your lifestyle. There are of course some things that are difficult to change, but you can take steps that may help you to keep things in perspective. There are many books available on stress management, but you may find the following points helpful:

- Try to see your problems in context.

When you're going through a stressful period, it's easy to over-react, emphasizing the negative and forgetting the positive. At such times it is useful to identify the specific situations that you are finding most difficult and to discuss them with family or friends.

- Deal with each specific problem separately – rather than trying to reorganize your whole life in one go!

It might be helpful to write your problems down, laying out the advantages and disadvantages of a particular situation. This should help you to see each problem more clearly.

- In reappraising your lifestyle, try to work out your priorities.

Where do the needs of family and friends rate alongside such things as work and leisure interests? Is the time you spend at work out of balance with the time you spend at home? Are you trying to do everything yourself instead of delegating work to other people? Are you placing your health too low down on the list of priorities? These are the sort of questions to examine and discuss with your family, friends, and workmates.

- Examine the balance of your time allocation between work and leisure pursuits.

Playing hard can be a valuable counterpart to working hard, whether it is physical play – as in sport – or other leisure pursuits such as cooking, going to the theatre or cinema, attending evening classes, or gardening. It helps to keep work in perspective, and shutting off from work for a period will enable you to return to it in a refreshed and less tense frame of mind.

- Try to keep some time each day just for yourself.

Give yourself some space for activities of your own choice, even if you use the time simply for a period of quiet reflection or relaxation. You will probably already have your own favourite 'treats' – such as having a warm bath, getting someone to massage your neck and shoulders, or simply listening to your favourite music. There are also some other techniques to help you relax, and we will now look at two of these.

Deep breathing

In stressful situations we often tend to breathe rapidly and take in short, shallow breaths. To counteract this tendency and to help to reduce tension, it is useful to practise deep-breathing exercises. You can practise them anywhere, but preferably sitting in a comfortable position and without too many distractions – just shut your eyes and begin by taking in a long deep breath through your nose until you feel that you have filled your lungs to capacity. Then hold your breath for a few seconds before letting it out very slowly and gently through your mouth. Don't try to expel it, just let it flow out easily and naturally. When you feel your lungs are empty, wait a couple of seconds and then breathe in again in the same way. Repeat the sequence until you begin to feel more relaxed.

Some people find that it helps to relax them more if they picture peaceful scenes while doing this deep breathing. You might, for example, imagine the clouds sailing slowly across a clear blue sky on a warm, lazy summer's afternoon, or the sight and sound of the waves breaking on the beach (to the rhythm of your breathing). Instead of one setting, you could imagine that you are following a favourite walk, taking in the sounds, sights, and scents of the countryside as you go. This exercise (with or without deep breathing) can also be a good one for helping you to get off to sleep at night should this be a problem.

Progressive relaxation

This exercise aims to relax different sets of muscles progressively. Each set of muscles is first tensed up and then relaxed, working in sequence from the toes to the head. Tensing up the muscles enables you to recognize the feelings of tension in the different parts of your body, and consequently to understand more clearly what it is you are trying to remove! It is a particularly effective exercise when lying on your back in bed (you'll drop off to sleep in no time!); but you can do it in other comfortable positions, such as sitting in a chair, or even sitting in your parked car when you're having a service station break on a long motorway journey!

First shut your eyes and concentrate on tensing up your toes and feet, and then relax them. Aim to get a feeling of heaviness in your feet, the feeling that they are totally relaxed. If you don't get that feeling with your first tense-and-relax attempt, try it again. Then move on to your legs. Again tense up the muscles and then relax; and do the same with your buttocks. Now move on to the muscles in your abdomen, followed by your hands and arms – squeeze your hands together and make the whole arm tense and then relax. Follow this by tensing up the muscles in your neck and shoulders, and then relax them; and finally, screw up the whole of your face, and then relax it, blowing out air from your mouth as you do so. If you're using the technique to help you to get off to sleep, you could follow this with the 'peaceful scene' scenario already described under the deep-breathing technique.

Deep breathing and progressive relaxation are only two of a range of approaches that can be used in reducing stress. There are numerous others – from 'stroking' and 'massage' techniques, to meditation and yoga. With a gentle stroking technique, for example, you will find that you can reduce forehead tension quite effectively by rubbing your temples in a very gentle circular motion with your index and middle fingers. A foot massage is also a very relaxing form of massage. It's a matter of finding what works for you, and then using it to soothe away the tensions.

Smoking

The many dangers of smoking have already been stressed in Chapter 3, so there is no need to repeat them here. Without a doubt, smoking has a detrimental effect on blood fat levels including cholesterol. Therefore, anyone wishing to avoid the danger of heart disease must find a way of giving up smoking.

How to stop smoking and stay a non-smoker

In any lifestyle change, a number of stages are involved. In stopping smoking, we will call the stages (1) getting ready to stop; (2) planning a non-smoking strategy; (3) deciding when to stop; and (4) staying stopped!

(1) Getting ready to stop

In some ways, getting ready to stop is the most important part of the battle. For people who have been smoking for several years, there is often a reluctance to break a habit that has become part of their lifestyle. They know they ought to stop, but they can't quite convince themselves that they really want to. And to stop smoking successfully, it is necessary to want to stop and to believe that it is possible to stop.

So the first step is to convince yourself that it makes sense to stop smoking. The following points might be helpful:

- Look at the stark facts about smoking related problems, and think of the possible consequences that smoking can inflict on you and your family.
- Discuss things with people who support your decision to stop and are willing to help you.
- Work out the savings you would make by giving up smoking, and look at ways in which you could spend the money on improving your lifestyle.
- Find someone else who is keen to stop smoking, and work together on preparing yourselves for the change.

Whatever preparation you make it is important that you build up a high degree of motivation – the nature of nicotine addiction is such that a half-hearted approach to stopping is doomed to failure.

(2) Planning a non-smoking strategy

Having reached the decision that you want to stop, you then need to devise a plan of attack. If you have managed to enlist the help of someone who is equally determined to stop smoking, devise your strategy together. Because of the physical dependency on nicotine, you are at times likely to feel a powerful need to smoke (especially during the first couple of weeks or so), but often the desire for a cigarette is triggered off purely by habit. Your hands will reach for the cigarette packet and you will feel distinctly ill at ease in trying to resist the well-worn sequence of events from taking the cigarette out of the packet, to lighting it, and taking your first puff. So you have to be prepared for this part of the battle, and plan your defensive strategies accordingly. There are some useful agencies and booklets that can provide detailed help on stopping smoking, and some of these are listed in the Useful Addresses section on page 121. Here are one or two suggestions that might set you off on the right lines:

- Plan to change your routines so that you don't put yourself in cigarette smoking settings, e.g. if you always have a cigarette in front of the television after dinner, break the habit by doing something different (perhaps go out for a short walk).
- Find some edible (and preferably not too fattening) substitutes for the cigarette, e.g. munch a carrot or celery stick, or chew a piece of sugar-free gum.
- If you're a heavy smoker, plan to cut down as much as you can before you start the real campaign and reduce the amount of smoke inhaled.
- Keep a daily 'smoking diary' before giving up, so that you can see exactly when and where you tend to light up; note down how much you spend per day on smoking.
- Brief any 'supporters' of your intentions, and tell them the exact day that you plan to stop smoking so that you'll feel a sense of commitment to them.
- Decide against allowing yourself the odd cigarette as a reward for doing so well – this is a recipe for disaster!
- Plan to keep busy (perhaps take up a new hobby), so you have less time to miss cigarettes.
- Select a special jar for 'smoking money', in which each day you can put the equivalent amount of money you would have spent on cigarettes.

For most people, these sorts of tactics should help a lot. You may have a few withdrawal symptoms while your body is getting used to its healthier lifestyle, but these symptoms fade in a week or so in most cases.

For those smokers with a high degree of physical dependence, though, the process might not be so straightforward. In such situations, some form of nicotine-replacement therapy (e.g. in chewing-gum or skin patch form) might be worth considering. Your GP will be able to advise about this.

(3) Deciding when to stop

Once you have prepared yourself for the battle, the next step is to name the 'quit day' and let your supporters know. It's a good idea to remove (at least from view if not altogether) all objects associated with your smoking, such as lighters and ashtrays, so that you are starting off your first non-smoking day in a fresh, new 'non-smoking' environment. Perhaps plan some special activities on your first day – so that you are physically removed from your usual smoking environments – and try to think yourself into the frame of mind in which you become a non-smoker who doesn't have any need to smoke (rather than a smoker who is trying not to smoke). If you get strong cravings, try the sort of deep-breathing exercises described on page 85. Finally, give yourself some sort of treat at the end of the day as a reward for not smoking.

(4) Staying Stopped!

Sometimes smokers manage well on the first non-smoking day, and perhaps for even a week or more. Then they succumb to the notion that they've 'cracked it', and that the odd cigarette now and then won't matter. This is the fatal and all too frequent error that failed quitters have regularly fallen into; and once back in the old smoking routine, it sometimes becomes even more difficult to give up again. Another useful word of advice is to beware of the line of argument that suggests that you're getting a bit overweight as a non-smoker, and that this is really worse for you than the smoking! This is a nice bit of smoking rationalization, and one to be dismissed by reference to the fact that weight gain after stopping smoking is usually only temporary. Once your body has reached some sort of equilibrium again after overcoming its addiction to nicotine, any excess weight gain will gradually tend to fall away. For those smokers who have started to look drawn and prematurely wrinkled as a result of their unhealthy smoking lifestyle, the weight gain may simply represent a return to fitness and the re-emergence of a healthy body. For the majority of new non-smokers, and particularly those who have persevered beyond the initial week or so, each day will bring added benefits and an overriding sense of achievement. There may be a bit of sadness too, because you may feel that you've lost an 'old friend' – but the more you feel some of the unexpected rewards of non-smoking (e.g. the return to tasting foods as they really are, and the pleasure of opening the window and taking a deep breath of the fresh morning air without coughing up your lungs afterwards!), the more you will see the 'friend' as an enemy in disguise.

Finally, to help you stay a non-smoker, keep the following points in mind:

- Take one day at a time, and keep rewarding yourself for getting through each day without smoking (don't think about the days or weeks ahead).
- Remember that each day without smoking, staying a non-smoker gets easier and easier.
- Persevere as much as possible with the policy of avoiding situations that are associated with your old smoking habits (it won't be for ever – but until you've really cracked the habit avoid inviting temptation).
- Try to anticipate stressful occasions and prepare for the possibility that these will push you towards the comfort of your old smoking habit – get your substitutes ready in good time (carry some chewing-gum or boiled sweets with you for emergencies!).
- Don't forget to keep filling up your 'non-smoking reward' jar – count the money and enjoy your treats!

Case study VAL

Val, 37, has a bit of a weight problem – 'well rounded and cuddly', as her husband put it. She enjoys eating, smokes ten cigarettes a day, and doesn't like the sound of exercise. She's never liked sport, although she likes watching wrestling on television. She hates hospitals and anything 'medical', but she'd been rushed off to hospital earlier in the year with severe pains in her upper abdomen and at the top of her back, under her right shoulder blade. She thought she was having a heart attack, and was very frightened.

In the end, it turned out that it wasn't a heart attack. It was gallstones, and she had to have her gall bladder removed. She was amazed at how well she coped with the operation. The surgeons used the 'keyhole' technique – they did it by making a little hole in the abdomen, inserting a catheter with a tiny camera on it, then removing the gall bladder – all by remote control, directing the operation by watching it on a television set in the operating theatre! She was up and about a few hours after the operation, and only stayed in hospital for a couple of days.

As a result of tests carried out before the operation, however, the doctors found that her blood pressure was a bit on the high side (148/90 mm Hg) and her total cholesterol level was in the 'high-risk' category (about 7.5 mmol/1). She also came into the 'obese' range when her Body Mass Index (BMI) was calculated. She was only about 5 ft (1.52 ms) without shoes, but she weighed 11 st 3 lb (about 71 kg). She was given an appointment to see a dietitian to discuss approaches to improving her BMI, and reducing her blood pressure and cholesterol levels.

The dietitian talked over Val's eating habits – mainly a non-stop nibbling of crisps and biscuits, or anything else that happened to be around during the day. They looked at a diet sheet together, and at the different sorts of food. In particular, the dietitian wanted Val to try to introduce more fruit and vegetables into the family's diet. She was also advised to eat plenty of foods like potatoes, pasta, and wholemeal bread, and to cut down on foods with a lot of saturated fat in them, like fatty meat, full-fat cheese, and full-cream milk. Oily fish, on the other hand, like salmon or mackerel, would be good for her. They worked out a few recipes for low-fat puddings, like oat-based fruit crumbles with custard made with skimmed milk, rather than the high-fat pastry pudding with cream that had been the family's main form of dessert.

As for exercise, Val thought she might go along with a friend once a week to the 'Keep Fit' group at the village hall. It wasn't really her idea of a good night out, but she accepted the doctor's advice that she ought to try to lose a bit of weight. She'd been informed that she had got at least five risk factors for coronary heart disease – she has a tendency to have high blood pressure, she smokes, has raised cholesterol, doesn't take much exercise and is overweight. Val had always thought that females didn't need to worry about heart disease – but apparently this wasn't so. Anyway, the gallstones episode had worried her stiff, and she promised she was going to take herself in hand.

Smoking was more of a problem. She always enjoyed a cigarette with a cup of tea, and she knew she'd find this difficult to give up. She thought her 'Keep Fit' friend might be willing to try cutting down with her, as she knew she couldn't do it on her own. And she did like the idea that her GP put forward: of putting the money she saved on buying cigarettes into a jar labelled 'smoking money', and then blowing it all on a special 'non-edible' treat!

She was also going to try chewing some sugar-free gum as a substitute.

On her next six-monthly check-up at the GP's surgery, she had managed to reduce her weight considerably. In fact, she was now down to 10½ st (about 67 kg). This new score moved her into the 'overweight' category rather than 'obese' one. She'd still a little way to go to reach the 'acceptable' range, but she'd made a great start, and she'd also won an 'improver's award' at the 'Keep Fit' club. Her cholesterol had gone down substantially too. It was now around the 6.3 mmol/1 mark – still in the 'moderate-risk' category, according to the nurse, but on its way down, as was her blood pressure.

She hadn't managed to fill up the 'smoking money' jar yet, but that was going to be her next big effort. She'd set a definite 'quit day' with her friend. They'd bought in supplies of chewing-gum, and they'd nobbled the 'Keep Fit' club members to keep an eye on them. In fact, the club had decided to initiate a new award scheme for members who managed to stop smoking, So Val was intent both on getting another award and having a rave-up with her 'smoking money'!

11

The use of drugs and other treatments in hyperlipidaemia

In general, it is only after diet and lifestyle changes have been tried that other forms of treatment come into play, and where drugs are considered necessary, these will be in addition to the dietary and lifestyle measures rather than instead of them. This combined approach tends to increase the effectiveness of the drugs, and results in a treatment dosage much lower than would otherwise be the case. According to most medical guidelines, drug treatment should only be considered for the following categories, listed in order of priority:

- People with existing coronary heart disease (or who have had cardio-vascular surgery) who have a total cholesterol level above 5.2 mmol/l, or LDL cholesterol above 3.4 mmol/l.
- People with multiple risk factors or genetically determined cholesterol problems (as in FH), who have a total cholesterol level above 6.5 mmol/l, or LDL above 5.0 mmol/l.
- Any other cases (including post-menopausal women) with levels greater than 7.8 mmol/l total cholesterol or 6.0 mmol/l LDL, and an HDL ratio of below 0.2 (see page 32).[1]

This doesn't mean that everyone in these categories will need drugs; some people will find that dietary and lifestyle changes do the trick without needing medication. Clearly, whether and at what stage the doctor chooses to introduce drug therapy will vary with each individual case. It's important also that the doctor's decision should be based on the information provided by a full blood-fats profile (i.e. including HDL and triglyceride levels as well as total cholesterol), since reliance on total cholesterol scores alone can sometimes be misleading. The realistic aim of drug therapy is to reduce cholesterol levels to one of the lower-risk categories. Where coronary heart disease is already present, the British Hyper-lipidaemia Association recommends that the aim (in terms of LDL level) should be a figure below 3.4 mmol/l. In the absence of heart disease, an LDL level below 4.1 mmol/l is suggested.

Different types of drug

A convenient way of discussing the different types of drug available is to group them under three main categories: (1) drugs that lower plasma cholesterol alone; (2) drugs that lower plasma cholesterol and triglyceride, and (3) drugs that lower plasma triglyceride alone.

1 Drugs that lower plasma cholesterol alone

The first of these types of drug are what are called *anion-exchange resins*. They are artificial resins that (like the soluble fibres that we discussed in Chapter 7) pass through our systems without being absorbed. Thus, they have the same effect as soluble fibre such as oatbran, binding the bile acids that have been squirted into the intestine from the gall bladder and liver, and thus preventing them from being reabsorbed. The knock-on effect is then that more of the liver's cholesterol is used up in trying to replace the 'disappearing' bile! These drugs can help to reduce LDL cholesterol by 20–30 per cent and increase HDL slightly, though they also have the effect of raising triglyceride levels. The two resins currently available are *cholestyramine* and *colestipol*. These may be used as the first form of medication for people with raised total and LDL cholesterol, such as FH sufferers.

Unfortunately, these drugs do have a few side effects, which some people find difficult to cope with. They are rather gritty powders that are mixed with water or fruit juice, and they can produce feelings of bloatedness, flatulence, and constipation.

Another drug that acts on cholesterol alone is probucol. Unfortunately, it reduces both LDL and HDL cholesterol, so is not generally considered as the first choice in the treatment of hyperlipidaemia.

2 Drugs that lower plasma cholesterol and triglyceride

There are three main types of drug in this group: (a) fibrates, (b) nicotinic acid (niacin), and (c) statins.

(a) Fibrates

There are four main fibrates currently in use: *bezafibrate*, *ciprofibrate*, *fenofibrate*, and *gemfibrozil*. It's not entirely clear how they work, but they have the effect of reducing triglyceride levels by about 50 per cent, increasing HDL levels by around 10–15 per cent, and, in most but not all cases, lowering LDL by 10–25 per cent.[2] The fibrates are usually the first-choice drugs for people with *hyper-triglyceridaemia* and certain other types of hyperlipidaemia, but not for those with FH or more general hypercholesterolaemic conditions, for whom *statins* (see below) are usually tried first.

Fibrates have received some adverse publicity largely because of the findings relating to an earlier version of the drug, called *clofibrate*. In long-term studies of its effectiveness, it was found to lower cholesterol levels by nine per cent and there was a 25 per cent reduction in non-fatal coronaries. However, in examining the statistics for overall death rate (which did not fall significantly), it was found that deaths from non-cardiac causes actually increased, a finding that has been put down to the effects of an increased incidence of malignancy and gallstone-related disorders. Clofibrate has now been withdrawn, and in a more recent trial with one of the later fibrates (gemfibrozil), the adverse effects were not observed. In general, these newer drugs are more effective than the earlier versions, they are well tolerated by patients, and have very few side effects.

(b) Nicotinic acid (Niacin)

Nicotinic acid (or niacin) is one of the B vitamins (vitamin B3), and is found in very small doses in some vitamin supplements and in foods such as wholemeal bread, yeast, nuts, liver and some breakfast cereals. As a treatment for raised cholesterol, however, you need much larger doses (in the region of 3–6g a day), and such large amounts must only be taken under medical supervision. In cholesterol-lowering terms, it is very effective, lowering total cholesterol and triglyceride and increasing HDL, but it has some inconvenient side effects. Apart from the fact that it can exacerbate glucose intolerance (and gout) and sometimes produce abnormalities of liver function, it also tends to produce side effects such as itching, rashes, and 'hot flushes'.

Because of these side effects, certain nicotinic acid 'clones' have been developed such as *acipimox*. These aren't quite as effective in lowering blood-fat levels as nicotinic acid, but they have fewer side effects and are generally better tolerated by patients. Nicotinic acid tends to be used as a 'second line' drug treatment, in combination with fibrates.

(c) Statins

The introduction of these newer drugs represents a major advance in the treatment of hyperlipidaemia. They can reduce LDL cholesterol by 30–40 per cent and triglycerides by 10–20 per cent, and HDL cholesterol is increased to a small extent. There appear to be very few side effects, and the drugs (*pravastatin*, *simvastatin* and *fluvastatin* are currently the major statins in use, with others in the pipeline) are well tolerated by patients. They are effective 'first line' drugs for use in cases of FH and other forms of hypercholesterol-aemia sometimes combined with low-dose resin therapy. The statins have been used in several large-scale research studies that have demonstrated the effectiveness of drug treatment for hyper-lipidaemia without showing any serious adverse side-effects. In the Scandinavian Simvastatin Survival Study (the 4S study), for example, the use of simvastatin was shown to prolong the life of men and women with raised total cholesterol who had already had a heart attack or suffered from angina. The study, involving nearly 4500 subjects, showed a reduction of nearly 40 per cent in the risk of heart attacks in the treatment group in comparison with the non-treatment group. Similarly, in the West of Scotland Coronary Prevention Study (WOSCOPS), lowering raised cholesterol with pravastatin in a sample of over 6500 men reduced the risk of heart attacks by over 30 per cent.

3 Drugs that lower plasma triglyceride alone

As we have already seen, omega-3 fatty acids are very effective in lowering triglyceride levels, and a special preparation (*Maxepa*) that contains some of these fatty acids can be prescribed in cases of severe hypertriglyceridaemia (raised triglyceride levels).

Some general comments about drug therapy

It must be emphasized that drug therapy should only be introduced once diet and lifestyle changes have been tried, since the therapy will usually have to be continued for a considerable period of time (often for life). It's important to remember also that the diet and lifestyle changes should be continued while on the drug therapy, and in particular, since all cholesterol drugs affect liver function, you need to make sure that your alcohol intake is kept to sensible limits. When medication is given under careful supervision, the success rate in adjusting cholesterol and triglyceride levels to reasonable risk levels is extremely good. Your blood fat levels will usually be checked after intervals of six weeks to three months and any side effects should be noted.

Sometimes, doctors have failed to inform patients of the side effects of various drugs, but there's little point in keeping patients in the dark about the effects that a drug might have on their bodies – and, in some measure, the patients have a right to know. After all, it is the patient's body, and he or she needs to be in a position to decide, in consultation with the doctor, what is going to happen to it. It is encouraging to see nowadays how doctor–patient relationships are beginning to change, so that treatment is becoming much more of a co-operative exercise.

One encouraging feature of the use of drugs to lower the blood fats is that such medication can actually reduce existing deposits in the arteries. Particularly marked reductions were obtained in a study combining the use of colestipol and nicotinic acid, and reductions have also been found in studies combining diet with various other cholesterol-lowering drugs such as statins. With the development of yet more effective drugs it is likely that such reductions will be demonstrated even more convincingly in future studies.

Other types of treatment for hyperlipidaemia

There are two other types of treatment that have been used in severe cholesterol problems that are not responding well to drug therapy (usually particularly difficult cases of FH). These are (1) partial ileal bypass and (2) the apheresis (plasma exchange) technique.

(1) Partial ileal bypass

In some cases, hyperlipidaemia is particularly difficult to control even after drug therapy has been introduced, and in such cases an operation called partial ileal bypass may be performed. This is a surgical operation that involves bypassing the end of the ileum, and so diverting the intestinal contents away from the sites of the absorption of bile acids.

It's not a particularly common operation in Britain, but has been used more widely in the USA where it has been shown, in a study of about 400 patients who had suffered a previous heart attack, to produce a sustained improvement in blood-fat levels, and to reduce the risk of death from coronary heart disease. However, it does have a high incidence of side effects. It hinders the absorption of vitamin B12, and thus the operation involves lifelong injections of vitamin B12 every three months. It is also associated with post-operative diarrhoea; this is usually controllable with drugs, but sometimes requires reversal of the bypass. In the research study described above, about five per cent of the research sample had to have the surgery reversed because of uncontrollable diarrhoea. Nevertheless, it is a good cholesterol-lowering procedure, and often very successful.

(2) Apheresis (plasma exchange)

Apheresis is a very specialized technique involving plasma exchange, during which the plasma is first removed so that the LDL cholesterol can be filtered out, and then replaced. It was first carried out in 1974 at the Hammersmith Hospital, London, and has since been introduced in research centres throughout the world. Its use is generally confined to the most serious cases of raised cholesterol, and especially for cases of homozygous FH (see page 39).

With homozygous FH, patients' treatment by apheresis can significantly prolong life expectancy, and it has also been used beneficially, in conjunction with drug therapy, in a study using mainly FH heterozygotes.

The pilot study combining the use of apheresis with lovastatin (one of the statins) showed that LDL cholesterol could be reduced by almost 50 per cent, angina was reduced, exercise tolerance improved, and there was evidence of a reduction of atheromas in at least one patient.

In a study at the Hammersmith Hospital, the use of apheresis with simvastatin was examined in comparison with drug therapy on its own (simvastatin and colestipol in this particular study). The findings suggest that both forms of treatment are effective in lowering LDL cholesterol and in stabilizing or reducing athero-sclerosis. However, the researchers concluded that apheresis should be reserved for the treatment of FH homozygotes who do not respond to drugs.

Case study PETER

Peter, 50, first discovered that he had FH in his late thirties. He'd gone along to his GP for the first time in years because he was feeling a bit breathless, and he'd also been suffering a few aches and pains in his back. Things had been particularly busy in the estate agent's office in which he worked, and he thought he was probably going down with a bout of flu. He was somewhat surprised, therefore, when the doctor, having completed his examination, sent him off to the hospital for a blood test.

The GP had remarked on the small yellowish lumps that Peter had on his eyelid and knuckles. He thought they could be produced by cholesterol deposits, but he wasn't certain. The GP did say, though, that if he was right, it might mean that Peter's blood cholesterol level was too high; and this, in turn, could be contributing to his breathlessness, since too much cholesterol can clog up the arteries and thus reduce the efficiency of the blood circulation in the heart and lungs. This stagnated blood flow can then lead to a build-up of fluid in the lungs, resulting in chest pain and, particularly if the problems are on the left side of the heart, to breathlessness.

His doctor's diagnosis turned out to be right. Peter's total cholesterol level on the hospital test was over 14 mmol/l, and when one of the lumps on his knuckles was analysed it was found to consist of cholesterol deposits. This didn't mean much to Peter at the time, but his doctor said the cholesterol score was a very high reading and that he had an excess of what he called the 'bad type' of cholesterol in his blood. He also explained that the lumps were, in fact, something called xanthomata, a finding which confirmed that he had almost certainly inherited a disease called familial hypercholesterolaemia. He did the usual run-through of the family history, and discovered that Peter's mother had died of a heart attack at the age of 52, and his elder brother had suffered a heart attack in his mid-forties. Both of them also had the same sort of lumps on their hands as Peter. It seemed likely, therefore, that they carried the same defective gene responsible for producing the excessive quantities of LDL, which had been found in Peter's full lipid analysis.

Peter was referred first of all to a lipid clinic, where he was put on a special low-fat diet together with two drugs, nicotinic acid (niacin), and a drug called colestipol, a version of one of the resins (cholestyramine). He had about 18 months of treatment on this basis, and coped very well with the diet and the medication apart from the fact that he found the nicotinic acid a bit embarrassing in the mornings. In fact, it gave his face such a florid appearance that his wife thought he must have been on the bottle before breakfast! Since it subsided before he left for work, though, he persevered with it and managed to get his total cholesterol down to around 8 or 9 mmol/l.

He thought he was doing quite well until the cardiologist at the unit gave him an exercise ECG – one in which his heart was checked out while he was exercising on a treadmill. The normal ECG had been OK, but this one threw up some odd results, and the consultant said he wanted to do an angiogram. This meant that Peter's coronary arteries had to be examined from inside by use of a small catheter that produced video pictures of the state of the arteries. The angiogram revealed that his coronary arteries were in rather a poor state. They weren't blocked, but the blood flow was severely restricted as a result of the build-up of atheroma plaques. Peter was advised that he would almost certainly have to have a bypass if the atherosclerosis got worse; or they might possibly try a balloon angioplasty in which a narrowed artery is dilated by inserting, and then inflating a tiny balloon. But for the moment it was suggested that he should try a different form of medication. He kept on with colestipol, but the nicotinic acid was replaced by one of the statins. 'People respond differently to different drugs', the consultant had explained, 'and although you've done well on the current mixture, we think it's worth trying a new mix now. We'll have a go with one of the statins if you're happy about that. They've been around for long enough now to know that they're remarkably free of side effects for most people, and they're showing up very well in research studies.' Peter was happy to go along with this advice, and with a new dietary programme that he'd worked out with the dietitian.

After a couple of years, Peter's cholesterol had dropped to around 6 mmol/l, and he noticed that the lumps on his eyelid and knuckles had got much smaller. His second angiogram also revealed that there had been no further increase in atheromas; in fact, there was some evidence of a reduction of atheromas in one of his badly affected arteries. For the moment his bypass could be put on hold, since the new diet and drug therapy seemed to be keeping his arteries in a relatively stable condition. He couldn't help reflecting, though, that if his FH had been picked up at an earlier stage, he could have started his fight back before the atheroma plaques had started to build up in earnest. 'It makes me angry when people pooh-pooh the value of cholesterol testing. It's the only way of finding out about FH or any other form of cholesterol problem; and the earlier you know about it, the better your chances are of treating it successfully. Somehow, we've got to start getting this message across.'

12

Countdown to healthy cholesterol levels: guidelines for action

This chapter summarizes the main features of a suitable diet and lifestyle for anyone with cholesterol problems. However, since these principles are applicable to a healthy lifestyle generally, this section is also a 'good food/good health' guide for the person whose health is unaffected by raised blood-fats. First, a mnemonic is offered to help you, and this is followed by questions that are often asked. Although there are rarely cut-and-dried answers, it is hoped that the information given will be of help.

The mnemonic to remind you of some of the key factors in healthy eating and to help you in coping with cholesterol problems is 'KEEP FIT & EAT WELL':

Keep to a diet low in salt and low in saturated fat (go for mono-unsaturates or polyunsaturates instead).

Exercise regularly – aim for at least 30 minutes' brisk exercise five days a week.

Enjoy an alcoholic drink, but keep it to sensible limits.

Pack up smoking, and plan ways of reducing stress.

Find low-fat substitutes for high-fat foods (e.g. make cheese-cake with quark).

Increase your intake of fruit, nuts, and vegetables (the anti-oxidant specials).

Trim the fat off meat and choose lean cuts for cooking.

Eat plenty of wholemeal bread, potatoes, rice and pasta; cereals (such as oats) and pulses (e.g. beans).

Avoid hidden fats, especially saturated – check the food labels for fat content.

Try skimmed or semi-skimmed milk instead of full fat milk, and keep to low fat cheese.

Wok-cook, grill, steam or microwave rather than deep fry.

Eat a variety of foods, with your meals spread out through the day.

Lower triglycerides, fibrinogen and blood pressure (and increase HDL) by eating oily fish.

Learn to cook the Mediterranean way, including the use of garlic!

Do I have to diet?

It's not so much dieting that is the key issue with cholesterol problems, but reducing the intake of saturated fat. You can eat extremely well, and there are a huge range of foods that are actually very good for you – like fruit, nuts, and vegetables, all of which have proven anti-oxidant properties.

But what's the point in dieting if cholesterol problems are all down to genetics?

Well, in the first place, they're not 'all down to genetics'. Our bodies are likely to be genetically predisposed to develop certain types of physical (and psychological) malfunctioning, but whether such malfunctioning actually materializes, or the extent to which it takes hold if it does develop, will depend to a large extent upon environmental factors. And one of the most important environmental factors in determining the extent of potential cholesterol problems is diet. A great many cholesterol problems, in fact, could be prevented altogether if more people adopted healthy eating patterns as part of their general lifestyle; and even in the most severe cases of familial hypercholesterolaemia, diet plays an essential role in controlling the condition.

I gather that women don't have cholesterol problems, so why should I bother?

Women do generally have better cholesterol profiles than men, probably as a result of hormonal differences. They tend to have higher HDL levels, for example, and their bodies seem to be capable of handling saturated fats better. However, the difference in average cholesterol levels between men and women isn't enormous, and you should remember that there is a wide range of individual differences in the sort of levels found among women. In fact, women can have seriously high cholesterol levels, and may have a substantial risk of coronary heart disease especially if they are smokers (and even more so if they are smokers and taking oral contraceptives). Moreover, post-menopausal women have higher average total cholesterol levels than men, and an increased risk of heart disease, though taking HRT can substantially reduce this level of risk. Women also seem to have about the same level of risk of FH as men. So if you're a woman, it's certainly worth bothering to have your cholesterol level checked, just as it is with men.

I lead a healthy lifestyle and eat healthy foods, so what's the point in checking my cholesterol?

This question can be answered best by pointing to the large number of people who have found that they *do* have cholesterol problems, even though they have what they consider to be healthy lifestyles and eating habits.

Sometimes, of course, what people think of as a healthy diet can be way off target when it comes to keeping blood fats in check. When the saturated fat content of the diet is examined, it can frequently turn out to be surprisingly high – so that the 'healthy' diet turns out to be anything but healthy in cholesterol-lowering terms! Even when the diet is relatively low in saturated fat, this still doesn't guarantee that there are no lurking blood-fat problems. Unfortunately, we often inherit slight imperfections in the way our bodies handle fats, and only a full blood lipid profile will uncover the extent of such problems. Having a cholesterol test will help you check whether you need to take further action; and having identified the problem, your diet can be 'fine tuned' to help deal with your own particular difficulties. And this is the key point – you can almost invariably help to reduce cholesterol problems by altering your diet.

What's the point in bothering about cholesterol at my age (72)?

There's no doubt that the earlier you start to keep your cholesterol in check (e.g. by eating a healthy diet, low in saturated fat), the better your chances of avoiding heart disease. However, you can still reduce your risk of having a heart attack by lowering your cholesterol score at any age. (Details of risk levels for people of different age groups are given in Chapter 3, and for different cholesterol levels in Chapter 5.) In fact, it has been estimated that for people of 70 and over, a reduction in cholesterol level by as little as 0.6 mmol/l can reduce the risk of developing coronary heart disease by 20 per cent. What's more, you'll reap the benefit of such a reduction pretty quickly – mostly within a couple of years, and the full benefit after five years.

Can cholesterol be too low?

This is not really seen as a problem. There is a great deal of evidence that raised cholesterol is an important risk factor in coronary heart disease, but there is no evidence to suggest that it would be desirable to increase low cholesterol levels. It is true that some studies have found an association between low blood cholesterol and some illnesses (including cancer and depression), but this almost always results from the disease process causing the low cholesterol – rather than the other way round. The reported link between low cholesterol and suicide, for example, is explained by the tendency for depression to lead to poor eating habits, loss of weight, and a consequent reduction in cholesterol levels, rather than the low cholesterol causing the depression.

Low cholesterol levels confer a low risk of coronary heart disease, and there are very few situations where doctors worry about low cholesterol – unless it is linked to other problems such as eating disorders. Indeed in some places, such as rural China, the range of blood cholesterol levels has been found to be between 2.5 and 4 mmol/l, and these levels are not associated with an increase in diseases such as cancer. Something like 90 per cent of Japanese men have a total cholesterol level below 4.4

mmol/l, but their risk of cancer is no higher than that of American or Northern European men.

If I keep saturates low, can I have as much monounsaturated and polyunsaturated fat as I like?

The best way to lower your cholesterol is to modify the total fat in the diet – reduce the saturated and replace it with unsaturated, a mixture of monounsaturates and polyunsaturates. But it still needs to be kept within the guidelines[1], which are about 30–35 per cent total fat, with no more than a third of this (i.e. ten per cent if you take 30 per cent as the total fat limit) as saturated fat. This is the basis of the Step 1 diet (see pages 75–6).

For someone with an energy requirement of around 2,000 kcal (say an active middle-aged woman), this means keeping your total fat to within the range 67–78 g per day[2] (about 2¼ to 2¾ oz fat, or 10–12 tsp oil). For people with more serious problems who are following the Step 2 diet, this would mean restricting their intake of *saturated* fat to about 15 g (½ oz) or less per day.[3] And to get an idea of how easy it is to consume ½ oz of fat, it's worth remembering that lots of people spread this amount on just one slice of bread!

What's the best way to start changing my eating habits?

First, work out where the total saturated fat in your diet is coming from, and then modify that. It may be cheese, meat or processed meats, or the frying of foods. Probably fried food is the first thing that needs to go with the majority of people. You can still have (lean) bacon with an egg, but the egg should be scrambled, boiled, poached, or microwaved, and the bacon grilled. Two to three eggs a week are OK, because it's not the dietary cholesterol that's most important, but the saturated fat.

There are other very simple changes that can be made: changing from white to wholemeal bread, drinking skimmed milk, and following the Mediterranean diet (see Chapter 8).

Is a low-fat diet all right for children?

The low-fat diet is thought not to be quite so good for very young children in some respects. It's laid down that children under two should not have low-fat milk; if they're over two, they can have semi-skimmed milk, and if they're above five, they can have skimmed milk. A well-balanced, healthy, low-fat diet is fine after that age. The need for full-fat milk early on is because children need energy for growing; and because they've only got small stomachs, they can't eat a lot of low energy, high-fibre foods.

Do I have to do without cream and ice cream?

What you have to do is use brands that are low in saturated fat or find a suitable substitute. For example, there are several ice creams around that are very low in saturated fat, and you can use half-fat yoghurt, low-fat fromage frais, or quark as substitutes (see recipe for quark-based cheesecake in Chapter 13). A particularly interesting 'substitute cream' can be made by mixing low-fat yoghurt with quark or low-fat fromage frais. You can have water-based sorbets for sweet or custard instead of ice cream with stewed fruit (custard powder is virtually fat-free).

What about snacks and sweets?

In terms of fat levels, marshmallows, wine gums, and boiled sweets are all OK (as opposed to most bars of chocolate), but they are high in sugar, so they will not be all right if you have diabetes or hypertriglyceridaemia (or are concerned about rotting teeth!). Other suitable snacks are oatbran crispbreads or crumpets – which have hardly any fat in them provided you don't load it on top! And of course there is always fruit, a stick of celery or carrot, or some suitable nuts (see page 62).

What sort of cooking is best?

It's generally best to avoid deep frying. Grilling is a good substitute for frying; or, with vegetables, try steaming rather than boiling, which tends to leave the vitamins in the water. The microwave is also good for cooking fish and vegetables.

Any tips for shopping?

Yes – read all ingredient labels extremely carefully!

How does a cholesterol-lowering diet fit in with cooking for the whole family?

This diet is basically just healthy eating, so it's suitable for everyone – and a low-cholesterol diet certainly doesn't have to be dull. Try the recipes in Chapter 13!

13

Eating well on a cholesterol-lowering diet: some recipes

The recipes in this chapter are based on the principles of healthy eating already described in previous chapters, and they are therefore suitable for anyone – regardless of whether or not they have cholesterol problems. At the same time, the recipes aim to help people who are on lipid-lowering diets to increase their range of food choice. In particular, suggestions are offered for ways of baking cakes, buns, and biscuits with ingredients that help lower cholesterol levels, and for making very low-fat versions of traditionally high-fat recipes such as cheesecake. All the recipes are either virtually fatless or 'low fat', in contrast to the usual range of cookbook recipes. However, the total fat content for certain items (e.g. a whole cake) could be seen as quite high if eaten all in one go! The amount of fat you would eat in one or two slices of cake a week, on the other hand, is quite a different matter. You will find that if each cake or pudding is divided into 12–14 portions, a portion will contain about 1½ teaspoonfuls of oil/fat (equivalent to 7½ ml or 10 g); and each crunchy bar will have the same amount. One tablespoonful of the granola mixture contains about ½ a teaspoonful, as does each bun or slice of cheesecake or malt loaf; and one biscuit contains about a third of a teaspoonful.

Estimating the fat content of food portions

You can work out a fairly accurate estimate of fat content for each portion of food by calculating the total amount of oil in the recipe (not forgetting the 'hidden fat' in ingredients like nuts and oats), and then dividing this by the number of portions. To convert fat measurements to their equivalent in oil, it's useful to know that 1 g is roughly equivalent to 0.75 ml oil. For example, the fruity oatbran buns have 1 tbsp (15 ml) of olive oil, plus some (mainly polyunsaturated) fat from the walnuts (about 17 g) and the fat from the oatbran (20 g). The 37 g fat from the nuts and oatbran converts to about 28 ml, and this, together with the 15 ml of olive oil, gives a total of 43 ml. Divide this by the number of buns (15), and this gives 2.9 ml – or about half a teaspoonful of fat per bun!

Fortunately, most people don't require this sort of precision, but if your cholesterol problems do require very careful fat monitoring, you'll need the assistance of a dietitian or a nutrition book (such as McCance and Widdowson's *Composition of Foods*) to make the calculations. To help you estimate the amount of 'hidden fat' in each of the main fat-containing ingredients in the recipes included here, a reference table is provided at the end of the chapter.

The introduction of the fat *olestra* in the USA has aroused considerable interest from the food industry around the world. It offers the prospect of a substance which has the taste and cooking properties of traditional fats but it passes through the body without being digested. At the moment it is only licensed in the USA and its use is restricted to the production of snacks such as crisps. However, even this limited use is controversial and many nutritionists are strongly opposed to any further extension of its use at the moment since it has a number of substantial drawbacks (e.g. it tends to interfere with the body's ability to absorb certain vitamins and it can produce faecal urgency and diarrhoea). So, as far as olestra is concerned (and other possible fat substitutes) we shall have to wait and see how things develop. For the present, the main alternative approach adopted in these recipes is the use of unsaturated oils (rather than hard margarines or butter) in the baking process. Since the replacement of saturated fat by a monounsaturated variety has particularly beneficial effects on blood fat levels, I have tended to use a light olive oil in the recipes, but other unsaturated oils would work equally well, and some cheaper blended vegetable oils contain an equally high level of monounsaturated fat. For savoury dishes you could use the stronger-flavoured extra virgin olive oil which contains a particularly high concentration of polyphenolic compounds (see page 68).

Apart from making pastry (which tends to become rather solid!) you will find that you can often substitute 1 tbsp of oil (about 15 ml or ½ fl oz) for 25 g (1 oz) of margarine without having much effect on the quality of the end product. You can use olive oil in all sorts of recipes and I have found that it acts as a particularly good substitute for butter or margarine in making garlic bread. Similarly, if you wish to avoid egg yolks, you will find that you can either use the egg whites or substitute 2 tbsp of skimmed milk (about 30 ml or 1 fl oz) for each egg in cake recipes without affecting the texture too much. However, a sponge cake needs rather more milk (about 4 tbsp for each egg) to achieve a satisfactory texture, though it still remains denser and heavier than a sponge with eggs in it.

One suggestion for overcoming the 'solid pastry' phenomenon is to use filo pastry as an alternative, especially for providing a crispy pastry topping to a sweet or savoury dish or making a standard apple strudel – but brush the filo pastry with oil instead of butter! You can buy filo pastry already made up, and it is only about two per cent fat, with a tiny proportion of saturates – something like 0.4 per cent. For making pastries and crumbles you could also consider one of the new range of non-hydrogenated spreads. These are not usually suitable for frying but you can often use them in baking. You'll need to check each separate product for guidance on this point. The pastries or crumbles produced with such spreads are very appetizing but they do, of course, have a much higher fat content than filo pastry. It's also possible to reduce the fat content of cakes and biscuits by using prune pureé, made by blending dried prunes with water. You need to experiment with the amount of pureé required for different recipes, and the ratio of water to prunes. Replacing half the fat by an equal weight of pureé seems to work well in most cases, but you can often produce very good results with pureé alone. The fruit cake recipe on page 114, for example, works extremely well with a pureé made with 115g (4 oz) prunes plus 6 tbs (90 ml) water.

Another suggestion is that instead of cream you consider using some of the very low fat substitutes made with skimmed milk – like quark, low fat fromage frais, or yoghurt. You can experiment with various mixtures, but I have found that mixing some yoghurt with quark makes an excellent substitute for cream. If you want to make very low fat but creamy-tasting yoghurts, you might find a yoghurt maker worth a try. All you do is buy one very low-fat yoghurt and one small (500 ml) carton of skimmed, virtually fat-free, long-life milk. Then you mix the contents together thoroughly in a jug, having first sterilized the jug, yoghurt pots lids, and mixing spoon by rinsing with boiling water. Then pour the mixture into six empty yoghurt cartons, put their lids on, and place them in the yoghurt maker. Plug in, leave for four hours, and then take out the six new 'creamy' (but virtually fat-free) yoghurts and put them in your fridge. A simple and inexpensive pleasure, once you have invested in the yoghurt maker!

As far as savoury dishes are concerned, I have included fewer recipes of this kind, since the saturated fat content can usually be modified fairly easily, e.g. by sticking to lean cuts of meat, limiting the cheese toppings of dishes like lasagne to gentle sprinklings of low-fat cheese, and eating fish or vegetarian dishes. I have, however, offered one or two suggestions, such as a bean goulash and a TVP version of spaghetti bolognaise. TVP stands for 'textured vegetable protein' and is made from soya beans; it's available from supermarkets or health food shops along with a number of other similar soya-based products offering nutritious, virtually fat-free, alternatives to the traditional mince dish. (Soya beans offer a further possible benefit since there is some evidence that they may offer protection against certain forms of cancer.) You will also find that quorn mince will make an excellent non-meat bolognese and quorn chunks offer a versatile alternative to meat when making a curry or when having a barbecue.

The chapter ends with a few suggestions as to what one day's lipid-lowering menu might look like. However, you should bear in mind that the range of potential menus is enormous, and this is just one suggestion for a day's meals. If you find my selection doesn't fit in with your own tastes, just ignore it – instead, make up one of your own based on the healthy-eating principles outlined in the book. The important thing is to keep experimenting with different recipes – you can modify the ones I have included in all sorts of ways to suit your own tastes and circumstances. For example, you can lower (or increase) the fat and sugar content of recipes to suit your own preferences (and requirements), or cut out the sugar altogether and replace it, for example, with dried fruit. You can also play about with any of the other ingredients until you find a blend that suits you and your family. All the recipes in this chapter are based on this sort of experimentation, and I hope you find as much enjoyment from carrying out your own experiments as I have from mine. So eat healthily and enjoy yourselves – Bon Appétit!

RECIPES

Fruity oatbran buns

Ingredients
250 g (9 oz) oatbran
1 dssp baking
   powder
1½ tsp cinnamon
1 tsp mixed spice
25 g (1 oz) soft brown sugar
25 g (1 oz) chopped walnuts
½ eating apple, grated
1 tbsp (15 ml) olive oil
350 ml (12 fl oz) skimmed
   milk
85 g (3 oz) mixed fruit

Method
1 Oil bun tray(s) enough for
   15 buns.
2 Blend together oatbran,
   baking powder, sugar, spices
   and nuts in food processor or
   mixing bowl.
3 Add apple, olive oil and
   milk, and mix together.
   Allow liquid to soak in for
   1–2 minutes.
4 Add mixed fruit, and give
   final short mix without
   chopping fruit too much.
5 Spoon into bun tin(s) to
   make 15 buns.
6 Bake for about 15 minutes at
   220°C (425°F) Gas Mark 7.
7 Allow to cool before turning
   out.

Best frozen (or kept in a plastic
container or bag in the fridge).
They are delicious warmed up,
from frozen, for 40 secs or so
in a microwave oven.

(3 buns provide 50 g oatbran.)

Oaty crunch bars

Ingredients
1 tbsp (15 ml) malt extract
6 tbsp (90 ml) olive oil
1 tbsp syrup
85 g (3 oz) jumbo oats
140 g (5 oz) rolled oats
55 g (2 oz) sultanas
1 tbsp sesame seeds

Method
1 Oil base of 11″ x 7″ shallow cake tin.
2 Place oil, malt and syrup in a large saucepan.
3 Stir and heat gently for about a minute.
4 Add oats and sultanas, and mix thoroughly.
5 Press into tin and smooth down top.
6 Sprinkle sesame seeds on top.
7 Bake in oven at 180°C (350°F) Gas Mark 4 for 20 minutes.
8 Cool in tin for 5 minutes and then cut into 16 fingers.
9 Cool fully before removing from tin.

Currant and red wine biscuits

Ingredients
115 g (4 oz) wholemeal flour
55 g (2 oz) oats
2 tsp cinnamon
25 g (1 oz) flaked almonds
2 tbsp (30 ml) olive oil
Juice (3 tbsp) of ½ orange
2 tbsp (30 ml) red wine (or juice if preferred)
115 g (4 oz) currants

Method
1 Add oats, cinnamon, and almonds to flour, and mix together in food processor or mixer
2 Add oil, orange juice, and red wine
3 Mix together until mixture can be formed into a ball (add a little extra juice if necessary)
4 Add currants and mix briefly, but avoid cutting up the fruit too much
5 Roll out thinly
6 Cut into about 24 round biscuit shapes with cutter (2½″ diameter)
7 Using palette knife transfer to an oiled baking sheet and bake in oven at 190°C (375°F) Gas Mark 5 for about 15 minutes

Fruit cake

Ingredients

225 g (8 oz) wholemeal self-raising flour
1 level tsp baking powder (omit if using eggs)
55 g (2 oz) soft brown sugar
1 tsp mixed spice
6 tbsp (90 ml) light olive oil
2 eggs (or 4 tbsp skimmed milk)
6 tbsp (90 ml) skimmed milk
340 g (12 oz) mixed dried fruit (including mixed peel), preferably soaked overnight in 3 tbsp (45 ml) sherry or port
55 g (2 oz) glacé cherries, halved
15 g (½ oz) flaked almonds

Variation

Blend 115 g (4 oz) pitted prunes with 6 tbsp water into a pureé. Substitute for oil at Stage 3. (Use baking powder at stage 2 even if using eggs.)

Method

1 Oil and line 18 cm (7") cake tin.

2 Sift the flour, baking powder (if not using eggs), sugar and spice into a mixing bowl.

3 Add the oil, eggs and 90 ml (6 tbsp) milk. Beat for 2 minutes.

4 Add the fruit (leaving 6 cherry halves to decorate top). Mix thoroughly. Add a little more milk if necessary to obtain a dropping consistency.

5 Place in tin, sprinkle flaked almonds over top of cake, add pieces of cherry to decorate top, and bake in the oven at 170°C (325°F) Gas Mark 3 for 1 hour.

6 Turn the oven down to 150°C (300°F) Gas Mark 2, and bake for about another 30 minutes or until a skewer inserted into the cake comes out clean.

7 Remove from oven and leave to cool in tin for 1 hour. Then turn out.

8 When the cake is cold, store in an airtight tin for at least one day before cutting.

Sponge cake

Ingredients
170 g (6 oz) self-raising flour
115 g (4 oz) caster sugar
1 tsp baking powder
6 tbsp (90 ml) olive oil
2 tbsp (30 ml) skimmed milk
2 eggs
1 tbsp hot water
25 g (1 oz) flaked almonds

Method
1 Mix together all dry ingredients in food processor or mixer.

2 Add oil, milk, eggs and hot water, and beat for about 1 minute in food processor or 2 minutes at high speed in mixer.

3 Place mixture in two oiled 7" round sponge baking tins.

4 Bake in oven at 180°C (350°F) Gas Mark 4 for about 20 minutes.

5 Allow to cool for 5 minutes before turning out on to wire rack.

6 Fill with jam or other filling to choice. If making a lemon sponge, add 1 tbsp lemon juice instead of hot water and add zest of lemon to sponge mixture.

For an egg-free alternative, try making lemon or orange sponge slices. Use the method above, but add the zest of 1 lemon or ½ orange and two tbsp juice (instead of the hot water), and replace eggs by 8 tbsp milk. Place mixture in oiled 11" x 7" baking tray and sprinkle flaked almonds on top. Will take about twice as long to bake as the sponge cake. Cut into slices.

Spaghetti bolognaise (with TVP)

Ingredients
2 × 400 g (14 oz) tins of
  chopped tomatoes
1 carrot
1 stick of celery
1 onion, chopped
2 tbsp TVP mince
2 tbsp tomato purée
1 garlic clove, crushed
1 tsp dried oregano
2 tbsp red wine
pepper
225–340 g (8–12 oz) spaghetti

Variation
Use 235 g of quorn mince
  instead of TVP.

Method
1 Finely chop carrot, celery,
  and onion, and add tins of
  tomatoes, or blend all these in
  food processor.

2 Transfer to pan and add TVP
  mince, garlic, wine, tomato
  purée, and herbs.

3 Bring to boil and cook gently
  for about 1–1¼ hours, or until
  vegetables are tender.

4 Cook spaghetti separately in
  boiling water.

5 Drain spaghetti and serve
  with mango chutney and side
  salad.

  Serves 4 people.

Sardine paté

Ingredients
1 tin sardines
1 dssp low-fat fromage
  frais, to taste
1 tsp lemon juice
pepper

Method
1 Mix together fromage frais
  and sardines (for variety, tuna
  or smoked haddock make
  good alternatives).

2. Add lemon juice and pepper.

3. Garnish with watercress.

4 Serve with toast or
  crispbread.

Bean goulash

Ingredients
1 onion, chopped
1 clove garlic, crushed
1 tbsp (15 ml) olive oil
1 tbsp (25 g/1 oz) wholemeal
  flour
1 heaped tbsp paprika
225 g (8 oz) courgettes, sliced
2 carrots, sliced
1 sliced red pepper
1 × 400 g (14 oz) tin of
  tomatoes
275 ml (½ pt) vegetable stock
1 × 400 g (14 oz) tin haricot
  or kidney beans
2 tbsp (30 ml) tomato purée
2 tbsp (30 ml) red wine

Variation
(Bean goulash with
  dumplings)

Ingredients for dumplings
4 heaped tbsp S-R flour
1 tsp mixed herbs
1 tbsp olive oil
8 tbsp water

(Mix together flour and herbs
and then add oil and water to
make a paste. Drop
tablespoon-size portions into
casserole at stage 7. Makes 6
small dumplings.)

Method
1 Heat oil in flame-proof
   casserole dish.

2 Add onion and garlic; cover
   and cook gently until soft.

3 Stir in flour and paprika.

4 Add courgettes, carrots, and
   pepper; stir the mixture, so
   that the vegetables are well
   coated with the flour and
   paprika. Cook for 2 minutes.

5 Add tomatoes, wine, stock,
   and purée.

6 Cook at 350°F (180°C) Gas
   Mark 4 for 55 minutes, or
   until vegetables are soft.

7 Add beans to casserole and
   cook for a further 10 minutes

8 Serve with baked potatoes in
   their jackets.

Serves 6 people.

Apricot cheesecake

Ingredients

55 g (2 oz) plain flour
25 g (1 oz) oats
25 g (1 oz) soft brown sugar
1 tsp cinnamon
15 g (½ oz) flaked almonds
1 tbsp (15 ml) light olive oil
1 tbsp orange juice
1 tbsp (15 ml) red wine (or use more orange juice if preferred)
1 carton 250 g (9 oz) quark
½ of 150 g carton low-fat yoghurt (approx 3 oz)
2 tsp honey
zest and juice (2 tbsp) of half an orange
115 g (4 oz) chopped ready-to-eat apricots

Method

1 Wipe round 7″ flan case with oil

2 Blend together flour, oats, sugar, cinnamon and almonds (but leaving a few for decorating the top of the cheesecake) in food processor or mixer

3 Add oil, juice of ½ orange, and wine

4 Mix together so that it forms a large ball

5 Roll out flat on a floured surface so that it will cover the bottom and sides of the flan case; trim off any excess with a sharp knife

6 Bake blind for 15 minutes at 190°C (375°F) Gas Mark 5

7 Allow to cool, and prepare the filling while flan is cooling

8 Mix together quark with yoghurt, honey, chopped apricots (leaving a few pieces to decorate top of cheesecake), and juice and zest of half an orange

9 Spoon mixture into flan case

10 Decorate top with spare apricots and the remaining flaked almonds. Turn out on to a serving plate

11 Divide into 8 slices

Granola

Ingredients
3 tbsp (45 ml) olive oil
2 tbsp (30 ml) honey
115 g (4 oz) jumbo oats
55 g (2 oz) oatbran
55 g (2 oz) bran flakes
(lightly crushed)
55 g (2 oz) mixed nuts
55 g (2 oz) sunflower seeds
1 tsp cinnamon

Method
1 Melt oil and honey in saucepan

2 Mix together rest of ingredients in a mixing bowl

3 Add oil and honey and mix together

4 Spread out on to a lightly oiled baking tray

5 Bake for 20 minutes at 190°C (375°F) Gas Mark 4, stirring occasionally

Use as topping for stewed fruit. Freezes well

Raisin malt loaf

Ingredients
285 g (10 oz) raisins
55 g (2 oz) soft brown sugar
2 tbsp malt extract
275 ml (½ pt) cold tea
55 g (2 oz) chopped walnuts
1 egg, beaten (or 2 tbsp milk)
120 ml (4 fl oz) milk
400 g (14 oz) wholemeal self-raising flour

Method
1 Place raisins, sugar, malt extract, and cold tea in a bowl

2 Stir and leave to soak overnight

3 Prepare a 2 lb loaf tin by wiping inside with oil

4 Mix in milk, eggs (or extra milk), flour and chopped walnuts and put mixture in tin

5 Place in pre-heated oven at 170°C (325°F) Gas Mark 3 for 1–1¼ hours

MENU IDEAS FOR ONE DAY

Breakfast
Fruit juice
Oat-based muesli or porridge
with fruit (e.g. stewed apricots)
Slice of wholemeal bread or
toast, thinly spread with
marmalade
Tea or coffee (instant or filtered)

Mid-morning
Tea/coffee with fruity oatbran
bun

Lunch
Mineral water
Half grapefruit
Cottage or low-fat cheese, or
sardine/tuna paté with salad
Baked potato in jacket or
wholemeal roll/crispbread

Mid-afternoon
Tea/coffee with currant and red
wine biscuit or fruity oatbran bun

Evening meal
Wholemeal roll
Vegetable soup
Fish or lean meat,
potatoes and vegetables
OR
Vegetable dish such as bean
goulash

Stewed fruit with granola topping
and quark/yoghurt cream
Glass of red wine or grape juice

Supper
Hot drink (e.g. low-fat drinking
chocolate) using skimmed milk
Crispbread, toast, or fruity
oatbran bun

Analysis of 'hidden fat'-containing ingredients with at least one per cent fat content

Fat content per 100 g

Bran flakes	2.3 g	Almonds*	55.8 g
Flour	2.2 g	Hazelnuts*	63.5 g
Fromage frais (low-fat)	4.0 g	Mixed nuts*	54.1 g
Oats	4.8 g	Sesame seeds†	58.0 g
Oatbran	8.0 g	Sunflower seeds†	47.5 g
Yoghurt (low-fat)	1.0 g	Walnuts†	68.5 g

* Mainly monounsaturated   † Mainly polyunsaturated

Useful addresses

HEART UK (formerly Family Heart Association)
7 North Road
Maidenhead
Berks SL6 1PE
Tel: 01628 628638
www.heartuk.org.uk

HEART UK provides a valuable support and advisory service. It also offers a range of fact sheets, leaflets and books on the management of cholesterol and other coronary risk factors.

Alcohol Concern
Waterbridge House
32-36 Loman Street
London SE1 0EE
Tel: 020 7928 7377
www.alcoholconcern.org.uk

Alcoholics Anonymous (AA)
PO Box 1
Stonebow House
Stonebow
York YO1 2NJ
Tel: 01904 644026
www.alcoholics-anonymous.org.uk

Action on Smoking and Health (ASH)
102 Clifton Street
London EC2A 4HW
Tel: 020 7739 5902

Coronary Prevention Group
2 Taviton Street
London WC1H 0BT
Tel: 020 7927 2125
www.healthnet.org.uk

The British Heart Foundation
14 Fitzhardinge Street
London W1H 6DH
Tel: 020 7935 0185
www.bhf.org.uk

The Health Development Agency
7th Floor
Holborn Gate
330 High Holborn
London WC1V 7BA
Tel: 020 7430 0850
www.hda-online.org.uk

Quit (smoking)
Ground Floor
211 Old Street
London EC1V 9NR
Tel: 020 7251 1551
www.quit.org.uk

National Dairy Council
5–7 John Princes Street
London W1G 0JN
Tel: 020 7499 7822
www.milk.co.uk

The National Dairy Council produces some useful Fact Files which include information on the relationship between cholesterol and coronary heart disease.

Glossary of terms

ABV

Percentage of alcohol by volume of drink.

Aerobic exercise

Type of exercise that involves an increase in oxygen consumption, e.g. brisk walking, cycling, and swimming.

Angina

Pain in the chest on exertion or when overexcited, caused by restriction in blood supply to the heart.

Angiogram

See entry *angiography*.

Angiography

A procedure for examining the coronary arteries by passing a small catheter into the heart. The resulting angiogram, the picture shown on a screen or in photographic form, indicates the state of the arteries.

Anti-oxidant

A group of nutrients (found in many fruits, vegetables and nuts, and also in red wine) that play an important role in keeping *cholesterol* in check, and in fighting many other disorders by counteracting the *oxidization process*. The anti-oxidant nutrients (beta-carotene, vitamins C and E, and selenium) help to prevent this and to counteract *free radicals* (see entry below).

Apolipoprotein

The name given to the *apoproteins* (see below) when they form part of the *lipoprotein* particles. They sit on the surface of the lipoproteins and can be used as a relatively straightforward method of estimating *lipid* levels. Apolipoprotein A-1 (or apoA-1) is used to provide an estimate of *HDL*; and apoB gives an estimate of *LDL*.

Apoprotein

A special form of protein that acts like a 'wetting agent', coating fatty substances known as lipids (one of which is cholesterol) and making them water-soluble. These protein-coated particles are then known as *lipoproteins*.

Atheroma plaques

The crusty deposits, consisting mainly of *cholesterol*, which clog up the arteries. This leads to *atherosclerosis*.

Atherosclerosis

A condition in which the arteries become hardened and narrowed, like 'furred up' pipes, by the build-up of *atheroma plaques*.

Blood pressure

The pressure of the blood against the artery walls. It is measured by the height in millimetres (mm Hg) that a column of mercury reaches when the blood pressure is checked.

BMI

Body Mass Index. A formula used to determine healthy weight/height ratios. Calculated by dividing weight (kg) by height (m)^2.

Cardio-vascular system

The heart and its related blood vessels.

CHD

Coronary heart disease (see below).

Cholesterol

One of the fatty substances (*lipids*) that is carried around the body in the blood. It is a soft, waxy substance, made for the most part in our own bodies (in the liver), utilizing substances derived from the fat in food that we have eaten. It is essential to the healthy functioning of our bodies (e.g. it forms an essential part of the membrane in every cell in our bodies), but in excess it can lead to the problems of *atherosclerosis*.

Complex carbohydrates Starches like bread, potatoes, rice, and pasta.

Corneal arcus A whitish ring formed by the deposit of *cholesterol* in the eye. The ring can be seen around the edge of the cornea, the normally clear 'window of the eye' that covers the iris (the coloured part of the eye) and pupil.

Coronary See under *coronary heart disease*.

Coronary angioplasty A procedure for dilating a narrowed coronary artery. Using X-ray control a tiny balloon is inserted into the artery, inflated and then withdrawn.

Coronary heart disease (CHD) Disease in which the coronary arteries become furred up, largely as a result of the build up of *cholesterol* deposits (atheromas). When a blood clot (thrombosis) occurs in a coronary artery, this deprives the heart muscle of blood and can lead to a heart attack, sometimes also called a coronary or *myocardial infarction*.

Diabetes Disease in which the body's glucose metabolism (i.e. its ability to convert the sugar from the foods we eat into energy) does not work efficiently. The process relies on adequate supplies of the hormone insulin, which is produced by the pancreas. In diabetics, this supply is either too small in quantity, or deficient in some other way.

Dietary cholesterol *Cholesterol* found in food such as egg yolk. For most people, however, it is the intake of fat (especially saturated fat) that is the most important dietary factor in determining levels of blood cholesterol.

124

Dyslipidaemia

A condition in which there is some abnormality in the *lipid* profile (includes, for example, low levels of *HDL* as well as raised lipid levels).

ECG

Electrocardiogram – a device used to monitor the electrical activity of the heart.

Familial hypercholesterolaemia (FH)

An inherited condition in which raised blood cholesterol (hypercholesterolaemia) runs in families. The gene responsible for FH produces defective *LDL* receptors, and this results in an accumulation of LDL cholesterol in the blood plasma.

Familial hyperlipidaemia

A collection of inherited forms of hyperlipidaemia, including *FH*.

Fatty acids

The constituents of fats; these can be divided into saturated and unsaturated varieties (the latter being either monounsaturated or polyunsaturated).

Fibrates

A collective name for a group of drugs derived from fibric acid and used in treating *hyperlipidaemia*.

Fibrinogen

A protein in the blood that helps to regulate the process of clotting. If levels of fibrinogen are raised, as in people who smoke, this leads to the blood having too high a level of viscosity (stickiness), and hence an increased risk of blood clots.

Free radicals

Chemical 'agents' produced as a result of normal cell activity in our bodies. They encourage the *oxidization process*, and have been implicated as harmful agents in a number of diseases including *hyperlipidaemia* and cancer. *Anti-oxidant* nutrients help to counteract their effects.

HDL   See *High density lipoprotein*.

Heart attack   See *coronary heart disease*.

Heterozygous FH   Form of *FH* in which the defective gene is inherited from one parent only.

Homozygous FH   Form of *FH* in which the person inherits two defective genes, one from each parent.

High density lipoprotein (HDL)   About a third of the body's *cholesterol* is carried in the form of *HDL* and two-thirds as *LDL* (see below); HDL is the 'good guy' in the cholesterol story, since it seems to act like a scavenger, collecting up excess cholesterol and returning it to the liver so that it can be reprocessed or turned into bile.

Hydrogenation   The process used to produce solid or semi-solid fats from liquid vegetable oils. It has the effect of converting the unsaturated fats to saturates, forming stearic acid, which is a saturated fatty acid (though converting to monounsaturates in the body), and some trans-fatty acids, which are treated by the body like saturates. A high intake of these trans-fatty acids can lead to an increase in the ratio of *LDL* to *HDL* cholesterol and an increased risk of *coronary heart disease*.

Hypercholesterolaemia   Raised levels of blood *cholesterol*.

Hyperlipidaemia   A condition in which blood *lipid* levels are raised.

Hypertriglyceridaemia   A term describing the condition in which blood *triglyceride* levels are raised.

Hypertension   Raised *blood pressure*.

Hypothyroidism Underfunctioning of the thyroid gland.

Ischaemic heart disease Another term for *coronary heart disease*; from the Greek word *ischaemia* (lack of blood).

Isometric Type of exercise involving 'straining' activities, like weight-lifting.

Kilocalories (kcal) Measurement of calorie values (as found on food labels).

Kilojoule (kj) The metric equivalent of *kilocalories*.

LDL See *Low density lipoprotein*.

LDL apheresis A specialized technique for treating people with severe forms of *familial hypercholesterolaemia (FH)* involving plasma exchange.

Low density lipoprotein (LDL) One of the two main cholesterol-carrying *lipoproteins* (the other being *HDL*); it is the 'bad guy' in the *cholesterol* story, since an excess of LDL cholesterol results in the linings of the arteries becoming furred up with *atherosclerosis*.

Lipids Collective term for a number of fatty substances in the body (including *cholesterol*); from the Greek word *lipos*, meaning fat.

Lipoproteins The tiny spherical particles whose central cores contain the *lipids*, with the *apolipoproteins* (the wetting agents) sitting on the surface.

Metabolism The process by which the body converts raw ingredients such as food and air for use in building tissues, providing energy, and generally maintaining the body and its functions.

Millimole One-thousandth of the molecular weight of *cholesterol* in grams. In

Britain, cholesterol is usually measured in millimoles per litre of plasma (mmol/l). In some other countries it is measured in milligrams per decilitre (mg/dl).

MRI
Magnetic Resonance Imaging: a radiological technique which produces images of the arteries and nerves.

Myocardial infarction (MI)
The situation in which a thrombosis in a coronary artery results in part of the heart muscle being deprived of sustenance and dying, unless the clot can be removed shortly after its occurrence.

Nicotinic acid (niacin)
One of the B vitamins (vitamin B3) used in the treatment of *hyperlipidaemia*.

Omega-3 and omega-6
Called the essential *fatty acids*, since a sufficient supply is required for healthy nutrition. Omega-3 fatty acids are obtained primarily from alpha-linolenic acid, and found in some vegetable oils such as soya bean and rapeseed, and in oily fish. Omega-6 fatty acids come mainly from linoleic acid, found in vegetable oils such as sunflower seed oil.

Oxidization process
The process that makes fat go rancid; and when this happens to *cholesterol*, it penetrates the artery walls and forms plaques more quickly. It is counter-acted by the *anti-oxidant* nutrients.

Partial ileal bypass
A surgical operation used occasionally in severe cases of *FH*.

Polyphenols
Anti-oxidants, found for example in red wine.

P:S ratio
The ratio of polyunsaturates to saturates in the diet.

Regression
Reduction (e.g. of *atheroma plaques*).

Risk factors
Any genetic or environmental factors that predispose a person to develop

128

certain diseases, or that are likely to result in a reduced life expectancy.

Statins

The collective name for a group of drugs used in the treatment of *hyperlipidaemia*. They work by inhibiting the enzyme HMG-CoA reductase, which is involved in the synthesis of *cholesterol*.

Trans-fatty acid

See *Hydrogenation*

Triglyceride

A *lipid* made by the liver or from the fat in foods we eat. It is an important source of energy. The body's production of *triglyceride* is stimulated by intake of fat and sugar (especially in the form of alcohol). An excess of this lipid may lead to an increased tendency for the blood to clot.

Type A behaviour

A behaviour pattern exhibited by people who tend to be aggressive and competitive, with an exaggerated sense of time-urgency. There is some evidence that the anger and hostility elements are linked to an increased risk of *coronary heart disease*.

Venepuncture sample

When a sample of blood is taken from a vein using a syringe, e.g. for a standard 'fasting' cholesterol test.

Very low density lipoprotein (VLDL)

The *lipoproteins* that carry *triglyceride* around the body.

Xanthelasma

Cholesterol deposits that appear as yellowish lumps on the skin at the corner of the eye or on the thin skin of the eyelids.

Xanthoma

(*Xanthomas* or *xanthomata* in the plural.) *Cholesterol* deposits appearing as yellowish lumps on the tendons, especially the Achilles' tendon above the heels, and on the backs of the hands and wrists.

Notes

Chapter 2

1 The word 'cholesterol' is, in fact, derived from *chole*, the Greek word for bile.

2 Because of their fatty consistency, lipids are not water soluble; and since the transporting fluid (blood) and the fluid in and around the cells that the lipids are trying to reach are both water-based, it is difficult for non-water-based substances like cholesterol to reach their destination. But our bodies have found an ingenious way of coating the lipids with special proteins (*apoproteins*), which act as a type of 'wetting agent' to make the lipids such as cholesterol water-soluble. These protein-wrapped lipids form tiny particles (the *lipoproteins*) which can then be transported successfully to the cells.

3 The cells have what are called 'LDL receptors' which bind (or 'catch hold of') the LDL and deliver its cholesterol into the cells. During this process some of the cholesterol will adhere to the lining of the arteries, and when the liver is producing an excess of cholesterol, these deposits increase and lead to atherosclerosis. The arteries become hardened by the formation of atheroma plaques (*athere* is the Greek word for porridge and *skleros* means hard), so in a way we could say that our arteries become like crusty, 'hardened porridge'!

Chapter 3

1 Creatinine is a by-product of the process in which protein is broken down and used by the muscles. It filters out of the muscles and is transported in the blood to the kidneys to be excreted in the urine. For some reason – and the link is as yet unexplained – raised levels of serum creatinine appear to act as a marker for increased risk of heart disease. Raised levels of homocysteine in the blood also appear to act as a similar marker. This problem can be counteracted by an increased intake of folic acid (found in foods such as green leafy vegetables and yeast extract) and research is in progress on the effectiveness of folic acid treatments.

2 Insulin dependent diabetes (also called Type 1 or juvenile diabetes) tends to appear during childhood. In this form of the disease the pancreas produces so little insulin that regular injections are required in order to meet the body's needs. Non-insulin dependent diabetes (also known as Type 2 or maturity onset diabetes) tends to become apparent mainly in middle age. This form of the disease is usually less severe than Type 1 and can be controlled by diet or diet and medication.

3 Pre-menopausal women also tend to have lower triglyceride and higher HDL levels than men and these also contribute to their lower risk profile for heart disease.

4 Oestrogen has the effect of lowering LDL and raising the 'good' HDL cholesterol.

5 Women who have had a hysterectomy (removal of the womb) do not need to take the progesteron component and so can gain full benefit from the protective effect of oestrogen.

Chapter 4

1 The British Hyperlipidaemia Association suggests that opportunistic screening is justified in all adults from the age of 20. The problem with such screening, however, is that people with potentially harmful conditions are likely to slip through the net. This is why, in the USA, it has been recommended that all adults should have their cholesterol *routinely* tested on a five-yearly basis. Health educators have backed up this approach with the slogan 'Know your number' in which the number is the total blood cholesterol measurement!

Chapter 5

1 Even posture can affect cholesterol measurement. The cholesterol level taken with the person sitting down tends to be lower than one taken standing up; and lower still if taken with the person lying down. Too prolonged use of the tourniquet when taking blood can also result in a raised cholesterol score. To promote consistency in measurement techniques it is usually recommended that the blood should be taken after the person has been sitting down for a minute or two, and the tourniquet relaxed before the blood sample is taken.

2 The cholesterol level can also be analysed (using clotted blood) in a fluid called blood *serum* in which case you may find the term *serum cholesterol* used to describe such measurements – but the cholesterol levels are comparable to those based on plasma analysis.

3 To convert mg/dl to mmol/l when dealing with cholesterol measurements multiply by 0.02586. Thus 200 mg/dl converts to $200 \times 0.02586 = 5.2$ mmol/l. For a rough conversion you can also divide the mg/dl figure by 39 or multiply the mmol/l figure by 39. When dealing with triglycerides the conversion factor is 0.01129 (or divide/ multiply by 89 for a rough approximation).

4 Sometimes a person may also be tested for a lipoprotein known as *Lp(a)*. This is very closely related structurally to LDL but its level in blood plasma is thought to be regulated independently. It may also, therefore, operate as an important risk factor and any measurement above 30 mg/dl would be considered to indicate high risk.

5 Although you will not necessarily be given a score for LDL cholesterol when your blood lipids are tested you can calculate a rough estimate of LDL level if you have details of total and HDL cholesterol, together with a triglyceride measurement. The formula is: LDL cholesterol = total cholesterol − HDL cholesterol − (Triglyceride mmol/l ÷ 2.19). So for someone with a total cholesterol level of 5.2, HDL 1.8 and triglyceride 1.5, the estimated LDL measurement would be $5.2 - 1.8 - (1.5 \div 2.19) =$ 2.7 mmol/l.

It should be noted, however, that the calculation only provides a rough estimate of the true LDL figure. The formula can be distorted by triglyceride levels and it is not applicable at all if the triglyceride figure is greater than 4.5 mmol/l.

6 This is a less clear risk factor for heart disease than cholesterol but it carries increasing risk if linked with low HDL or raised total cholesterol. There is also risk of acute pancreatitis at levels above 10 mmol/l.

7 Sometimes the calculation is reversed and the HDL score is divided by the total cholesterol score, then multiplied by 100 to give a percentage score. Using this ratio

measurement, the 'satisfactory' range of scores for both men and women is between 20 per cent and 50 per cent. So in the example given, the percentage would be $1.2 \div 7.7 \times 100 = 16$ per cent, and so outside the 'satisfactory' range.

8 Some pathological laboratories will measure what is known as apolipoprotein B (apoB for short) instead of LDL cholesterol; and apoA-1 instead of HDL. The measurement of apoB offers a relatively straightforward method of indicating the number of LDL particles present in the plasma (and apoA-1 indicates the number of HDL particles). Although some laboratories use these measurements routinely there is a lack of agreement at present about which are the most appropriate laboratory techniques for estimating apolipoprotein levels and this means that there are no generally agreed guidelines on risk scores. However, where the ratio of apoB/apoA-1 is given instead of LDL/HDL it is usually assumed that a ratio greater than 1.0 is likely to indicate high risk.

9 The Dundee Coronary Risk-Disk is available from Risk-Disk, CVEU, Ninewells Hospital, Dundee DD1 9SY, Scotland. Tel: 01382-632283.

Chapter 6

1 As we have seen, though, a person can also have a high risk level because of a *low* HDL level. So some doctors prefer to use the term *dyslipidaemia* (instead of hyperlipidaemia). The prefix *dys* stands for 'problems or difficulties with' and hence dyslipidaemia indicates lipid problems in general rather than those based on raised blood fats alone.

2 The World Health Organization has classified different types of hyperlipidaemia, including familial hyperlipidaemias, according to their main characteristics (see below).

WHO type	*Characteristics*	*Example*
I	(Rare) total cholesterol level typically greater than 6.5 mmol/l but very high triglyceride levels (like IV and V) and an excess of lipoproteins called chylomicrons.	Lipoprotein lipase deficiency
IIa	(Common) raised total cholesterol levels (in FH frequently in double figures, sometimes as high as 16 mmol/l or more); always with high levels of LDL.	Familial & polygenic hypercholesterolaemia and familial defective apoprotein B-100
IIb	(Most common) the same as IIa but with raised triglyceride as well as LDL.	Familial combined hyperlipidaemia (can also exhibit types IIa, IV or V)
III	(Rare) high total cholesterol (typically above 9 mmol/l) but normal or low LDL; triglyceride is raised but not as high as Types IV and V.	Remnant particle disease
IV	(Common) normal or raised total cholesterol, normal LDL but raised triglyceride (typically within the range 10 – 30 mmol/l).	Familial hypertriglyceridaemia

V   (Rare) raised total cholesterol, normal LDL but   (as IV above)
         raised triglyceride (as in IV).

Additional primary disorders based on HDL levels and listed by the British Hyperlipidaemia
Association:
         hyperalphalipoproteinaemia (with HDL levels
         above 2)
         hypoalphalipoproteinaemia (with HDL levels
         below 0.9)

---

3 In FCH, tendon deposits aren't present, raised cholesterol levels are not usually as high as in FH, and they don't tend to show up until people are in their twenties and thirties. In familial hypertriglyceridaemia the body produces very high levels of triglyceride. The condition can also result in crops of small reddish-yellow lumps appearing on the skin and in pancreatitis (inflammation of the pancreas).

Chapter 7

1 EPA stands for eicosapentaenoic acid and DHA for docosahexaenoic acid.

2 The total fat content in butter (and other spreading fats) is less than 100 per cent since they all contain a proportion of water – often around 15 per cent to 20 per cent though much higher in 'low fat spreads'.

3 This process also produces stearic acid (a saturated fat) but this is converted by the body into monounsaturated fat and does not affect blood fat levels adversely.

4 The levels of hydrogenated or partially hydrogenated vegetable fat can be seen by examining the food label under 'ingredients', and the nearer to the top of the list the hydrogenated fat is mentioned, the higher the content. The saturated and trans- fatty acids originating from the hydrogenated oil are included by some food chains on the nutritional label under 'saturated fats', but at present there is no requirement to list the percentage of trans-fatty acids separately.

5 They enter the bloodstream in the form of sugars, of which glucose is the most common; and although the 'available' carbohydrates are high in calories, they provide much less energy per gram than other food sources (3.75 kcal compared with nine for fat, seven for alcohol and four for protein).

6 This is the so-called P:S ratio. It has been suggested that a ratio of 1.0 (i.e. 1:1 or equal proportions of each) represents a reasonable balance between polyunsaturated and saturated fats.

7/8 A food described as a source of soluble fibre may also, of course, include some insoluble fibre, but it has the highest concentration of the soluble type. Similarly, foods described as sources of insoluble fibre may also contain some soluble fibre.

Chapter 8

1 Allicin is formed when an enzyme (alliinase) and an amino acid (alliin), which are normally separate within the clove, are brought together, and it is the allicin yield which is usually taken as a measure of the quality of the garlic.

2 200 mg of garlic powder is roughly equivalent to 0.6 g of raw garlic.

3 But there are quite wide differences in 'egg tolerance levels' which are probably genetically determined. In fact, some people appear to have an 'egg-eating gene' which results in the presence of a protein known as apo-A-IV-2 that allows the body to deal with large amounts of dietary cholesterol without affecting blood cholesterol level. This protein is a variation of the normal protein everyone carries (apo-A-IV-1) that affects the body's ability to deal with fats.

4 In fact, shellfish have some particularly good features – they are low in fat, and high in protein, vitamin B12 and several trace minerals.

Chapter 9

1 Body mass index (BMI) is calculated by the formula: weight (kg)÷height (m)^2. In general, a BMI rating of less than 20 means that you are 'underweight', 20–24.9 is 'acceptable', 25–29.9 'overweight', 30–40 is 'obese' and over 40 'severely obese'. You can also check whether you are at risk from being overweight by dividing your waist size by hip measurement. A high waist-hip ratio can be recognized by a distinct 'apple-shape' as opposed to the 'pear-shape' of a low ratio person! A ratio of more than 1.0 for men or 0.8 for women puts the person at increased risk of cardio-vascular disease and non-insulin-dependent diabetes (see page 17).

2 The following formula is used to calculate units of alcohol: % alcohol by volume (ABV) × size of glass (ml) ÷ 1000 = number of units. Thus a glass of wine with a relatively low alcohol by volume (ABV) value (say 8 per cent) in a medium sized wine glass (125 ml) would be one unit (8 × 125 ÷ 1000 = 1 unit). Whereas a glass of stronger wine (say 15 per cent by volume) in the same 125 ml glass would be nearly 2 units! (15 × 125 ÷ 1000 = 1.9 units) Sometimes you are offered advice on the unit value of a particular alcoholic drink (in a glass of specified size) on the side of the bottle.

Chapter 11

1 Or a total cholesterol/HDL ratio of more than 5.0.

2 The main exception to the LDL lowering effect is in patients with hypertriglyceri-daemia, where LDL cholesterol is already low. In such cases LDL may actually rise.

Chapter 12

1 Based on reports such as those produced by the UK Committee on Medical Aspects of Food (COMA) and the World Health Organization (WHO).

2 This is calculated by working out 30 per cent to 35 per cent of 2000 kcals and then dividing the result by 9 (the energy equivalent in kcals of one gram of fat).

3 Occasionally people with very severe blood fat problems may be advised to restrict their daily total fat intake to something like five teaspoonsful a day (25 ml oil or about 34 g fat). This would be the very lowest fat intake advised, however, since we require about that amount per day to provide us with sufficient levels of essential fatty acids and to ensure the satisfactory absorption of the fat soluble vitamins.

Index